a /08

GW00360421

Penguin Modern Po
VOLUME 13

Robin Robertson is from the north-east coast of Scotland. He now lives
in London and works in publishing. His collection *A Painted Field* was
published in Britain in 1997 and in the United States in 1998, and won
the 1997 Forward Prize for Best First Collection, the Aldeburgh Poetry
Festival Prize and was chosen as the Saltire Scottish First Book of the
Year.

Michael Hofmann was born in Freiburg in 1957 and grew up in England
and the United States. He studied English at Cambridge and since 1983
has lived in London as a freelance writer, reviewer and translator from
the German. Penguin publishes his versions of Wolfgang Koeppen's
Death in Rome and Franz Kafka's *The Man Who Disappeared (Amerika);* his
Rilke in English is forthcoming. He was recently appointed Visiting
Lecturer at the University of Florida in Gainesville. His three books of
poems, *Nights in the Iron Hotel* (1983), *Acrimony* (1986) and *Corona, Corona*
(1993), are published by Faber.

Michael Longley was born in Belfast in 1939 and educated at the Royal
Belfast Academical Institution and Trinity College, Dublin, where he read
Classics. For twenty years he worked for the Arts Council of Northern
Ireland in the fields of literature, the traditional arts and arts in education.
He retired in 1991. His collections include *Poems 1963–1983, Gorse Fires*,
which won the Whitbread Prize for Poetry, and *The Ghost Orchid,* which
was shortlisted for the T. S. Eliot Prize. A Fellow of the Royal Society
of Literature and a member of Aosdana, he lives in Belfast with his wife,
the critic Edna Longley.

The Penguin Modern Poets Series

Volume One
James Fenton
Blake Morrison
Kit Wright

Volume Two
Carol Ann Duffy
Vicki Feaver
Eavan Boland

Volume Three
Glyn Maxwell
Mick Imlah
Peter Reading

Volume Four
Liz Lochhead
Roger McGough
Sharon Olds

Volume Five
Simon Armitage
Sean O'Brien
Tony Harrison

Volume Six
U. A. Fanthorpe
Elma Mitchell
Charles Causley

Volume Seven
Donald Davie
Samuel Menashe
Allen Curnow

Volume Eight
Jackie Kay
Merle Collins
Grace Nichols

Volume Nine
John Burnside
Robert Crawford
Kathleen Jamie

Volume Ten
Douglas Oliver
Denise Riley
Iain Sinclair

Volume Eleven
Michael Donaghy
Andrew Motion
Hugo Williams

Volume Twelve
Helen Dunmore
Jo Shapcott
Matthew Sweeney

Volume Thirteen
Robin Robertson
Michael Hofmann
Michael Longley

Penguin Modern Poets

VOLUME 13

ROBIN ROBERTSON

MICHAEL HOFMANN

MICHAEL LONGLEY

ESSEX COUNTY COUNCIL
LIBRARIES

PENGUIN BOOKS

Published by the Penguin Group
Penguin Books Ltd, 27 Wrights Lane, London w8 5tz, England
Penguin Putnam Inc., 375 Hudson Street, New York, New York 10014, USA
Penguin Books Australia Ltd, Ringwood, Victoria, Australia
Penguin Books Canada Ltd, 10 Alcorn Avenue, Toronto, Ontario, Canada m4v 3b2
Penguin Books (NZ) Ltd, 182–190 Wairau Road, Auckland 10, New Zealand

Penguin Books Ltd, Registered Offices: Harmondsworth, Middlesex, England

This selection first published 1998
10 9 8 7 6 5 4 3 2 1

Copyright © Robin Robertson,
Copyright © Michael Hofmann,
Copyright © Michael Longley,
All rights reserved

The moral right of the authors has been asserted

Set in 10.5/13pt Monotype Garamond
Typeset by Rowland Phototypesetting Ltd, Bury St Edmunds, Suffolk
Printed in England by Clays Ltd, St Ives plc

Contents

Robin Robertson

New Gravity   3
Three Ways of Looking at God   4
Advent in Co. Fermanagh   5
Sheela-na-Gig   7
Static   8
The Flaying of Marsyas   9
Aberdeen   12
At Dusk   13
Visiting my Grandfather   14
Fireworks   16
Escapology   18
After the Overdose   19
Lithium   20
First Winter   21
The Break   22
Raising the Paint   23
Shot   24
Jack-in-the-Green   25
Hands of a Farmer in Co. Tyrone   26
Feeding the Fire   27
Moving House   28
Artichoke   30
Blind Man Eating Winkles   31
The Immoralist   32
Silver Lake, Vermont   33
From Camera Obscura   34
   'Through the open door, and the
     latticed window'   34
   The Flowers of the Forest   34
   Circus on Calton Hill   35

Four Views from the Camera Obscura 36
'Could I find your face, or mine' 37
28 Inverleith Row 37
'She put her hand on me' 37
Flags of Autumn 38
Four Views from the Camera Obscura 39
'When I think of the womb of my daughter' 40
The Gift of Tantalus 40
'This lobster vanity draws me' 40
Dumb Show, with Candles 41
'Desire becomes sorrow' 42
Sunny Memories 42
'I cannot always hold your hand' 42
Dead Centre, 1858 43
Edinburgh Castle (detail) 43
Four Views from the Camera Obscura 44
'With every step of hers towards the light' 45
'My daughter feels no fear' 45
The Royal High School 45
'I look in the mirror and see nothing' 45
Amnesty in the Garden 46
'Night breathes on me' 47

Michael Hofmann

Touring Company 51
First Night 52
Family Holidays 53
Boy's Own 54
Furth i. Wald 56
Nights in the Iron Hotel 57
Body Heat 58
Ancient Evenings 59
On the Margins 60
Changes 62
A Floating City 63

A Brief Occupation   64
Nighthawks   65
From Kensal Rise to Heaven   66
Open House   68
Between Bed and Wastepaper Basket   69
Day of Reckoning   71
The Machine That Cried   72
My Father's House Has Many Mansions   74
Author, Author   76
Fine Adjustments   79
The Late Richard Dadd, 1817–1886   80
Marvin Gaye   81
Freebird   82
Up in the Air   84
Wheels   85
Schönlaterngasse   86
From A to B and Back Again   87
Summer '87   88
Las Casas   89
Guanajuato Two Times   91

Michael Longley

Graffiti   95
The Ornithological Section   96
Odyssey   98
Words for Jazz Perhaps   100
The Rope-makers   102
Irish Poetry   103
Carrigskeewaun   104
Wounds   106
Kindertotenlieder   107
The Island   108
Weather   109
The Lodger   110
The Goose   111

Ars Poetica   112
Stilts   114
Architecture   115
Oliver Plunkett   116
On Hearing Irish Spoken   118
from Mayo Monologues   119
Mountain Swim   120
Meniscus   120
Dead Men's Fingers   121
Florence Nightingale   122
No Man's Land   123
The Third Light   124
Halley's Comet   125
The Shack   126
Ghetto   127
Stone-in-Oxney   130
Eurycleia   131
Trade Winds   132
Sitting for Eddie   133
Perdix   134
Spiderwoman   135
Ivory & Water   136
A Gift of Boxes   137
Chenac   138
The Dry Cleaners   139
The Fishing Party   140
Ceasefire   141
The Scales   142
The Mad Poet   143
After Horace   144

Acknowledgements   145

Robin Robertson

New Gravity

Treading through the half-light of ivy
and headstone, I see you in the distance
as I'm telling our daughter
about this place, this whole business:
a sister about to be born,
how a life's new gravity suspends in water.
Under the oak, the fallen leaves
are pieces of the tree's jigsaw;
by your father's grave you are pressing acorns
into the shadows to seed.

Three of Ways of Looking at God

1

A claustrophobia of sand and stone: a walled heat.
The light bleaches and curves like a blade, isolates
the chirr of crickets, seed-pods detonating,
the valley waiting in a film of flame.
A bird finds an open channel in the air
and follows it without exertion to the branch.

2

The sky is slashed like a sail. Night folds
over the shears, the dye, the docked tails.
We listen to the rumours of the valley:
goats' voices, gear-changes, the stirring of dogs.
In the green light, lambs with rouged cheeks
skitter from their first communion, calling for home.

3

Lightning flexes: a man chalked on a board, reeling,
exact, elementary, flawed; at each kick, birds flinch
and scatter from the white lawn.
The long trees bend to the grain of the gale,
streaming the dark valley like riverweed.
All night: thunder, torn leaves; a sheathing of wings.

Advent in Co. Fermanagh

Two chemists in one village,
side by side,
ours and theirs;
both specialise in cattle cures.
The greengrocer, meanwhile,
doubles as undertaker;
his potatoes
always hard and white,
beautifully laid out.

The town is bottle-shaped
and dressed for Christmas
in a morse code of coloured lights,
marginal snow
in crescents at the windows,
and on the sill,
in the holly's gloss
of red and starred green,
illuminating angels.

Leaning men on corners watch
the circumspect, the continent,
linking their way to church.
Then the mid-day angelus
opens the doors in the street
like organ stops,
for the pinched and raddled
in their penitential suits
pulling children out of doorways:
strings of hankies from a sleeve.

No one watches the soldiers
walking backwards on patrol:
the cellophane crackle of radios,
the call and answer
as they stroll, each cradling
a weapon like a newborn child.

Stooped under hangovers,
the pasty supplicants
file towards the priest
to say 'Aaah' for atonement,
and shuffle out, cowed,
in a cold sweat,
His Body
tucked behind the teeth.

Doors disclose them,
scribbling down the hill
for rashers and egg
and wheaten bread;
Guinness and Black Bush:
gifts for the back room
with the curtains pulled.

Sunlight glints
like mica schist in granite
on the huddled homes
as the rain comes casting down.

Stone circles of sheep
in the drowned field
watch helicopters come
dreaming over hedges:
horse-flies the size of houses,
great machines
for opening the air,
and shaking it shut.

Leaving an absence, a silence,
and a hatch of light
which discovers a door.
The town drunk emerges
gingerly from the bar,
amazed by the familiar;
patting his pockets,
blinking like Lazarus.

Sheela-na-Gig

He has reached her island by stones
pegged in swollen water,
through rain that has fallen for days.

He touches the welling mouth, the split stone;
she shows him the opening folds
where rainwater troubles and turns.

The rain slows, and stops; light deepens
at the lid of the lake, the water creased
by the head of an otter, body of a bird.

Static

The storm shakes out its sheets
against the darkening window:
the glass flinches under thrown hail.
Unhinged, the television slips its hold,
streams into black and white
then silence, as the lines go down.
Her postcards stir on the shelf, tip over;
the lights of Calais trip out one by one.

He cannot tell her
how the geese scull back at twilight,
how the lighthouse walks its beam
across the trenches of the sea.
He cannot tell her how the open night
swings like a door without her,
how he is the lock
and she is the key.

The Flaying of Marsyas
after Ovid

I

A bright clearing. Sun among the leaves,
sifting down to dapple the soft ground, and rest
a gilded bar against the muted flanks of trees.
In the flittering green light the glade
listens in and breathes.

A wooden pail; some pegs, a coil of wire;
a bundle of steel flensing knives.

Spreadeagled between two pines,
hooked at each hoof to the higher branches,
tied to the root by the hands, flagged
as his own white cross,
the satyr Marsyas hangs.

Three stand as honour guard:
two apprentices, one butcher.

II

Let's have a look at you, then.
Bit scrawny for a satyr,
all skin and whipcord, is it?
Soon find out.
So, think you can turn up with your stag-bones
and outplay Lord Apollo?
This'll learn you. Fleece the fucker.
Sternum to groin.
Tickle does it? Fucking bastard,
coming down here with your dirty ways . . .
Armpit to wrist, both sides.

9

Chasing our women . . .
Fine cuts round hoof and hand and neck.
Can't even speak the language proper.
Transverse from umbilicus to iliac crest,
half-circling the waist.
Jesus. You fucking stink, you do.
Hock to groin, groin to hock.
That's your inside leg done:
no more rutting for you, cunt.

Now. One of you on each side.
Blade along the bone, find the tendon,
nick it and peel, nice and slow.
A bit of shirt-lifting, now, to purge him,
pull his wool over his eyes
and show him Lord Apollo's rapture;
pelt on one tree, him on another:
the inner man revealed.

III

Red Marsyas. Marsyas *écorché*,
splayed, shucked of his skin
in a tug and rift of tissue;
his birthday suit sloughed
the way a sodden overcoat is eased
off the shoulders and dumped.
All memories of a carnal life
lifted like a bad tattoo,
live bark from the vascular tree:
raw Marsyas unsheathed.

Or dragged from his own wreckage,
dressed in red ropes
that plait and twine his trunk
and limbs into true definition,

he assumes the flexed pose of the hero:
the straps and buckles of ligament
glisten and tick on the sculpture
of Marsyas, muscle-man.
Mr Universe displays the map of his body:
the bulbs of high ground carved
by the curve of gully and canal,
the tributaries tight as ivy or the livid vine,
and everywhere, the purling flux of blood
in the land and the swirl of it flooding away.

Or this: the shambles of Marsyas.
The dark chest meat marbled with yellow fat,
his heart like an animal breathing
in its milky envelope,
the viscera a well-packed suitcase
of chitterlings, palpitating tripe.
A man dismantled, a tatterdemalion
torn to steak and rind,
a disappointing pentimento
or the toy that can't be re-assembled
by the boy Apollo, raptor, vivisector.

The sail of stretched skin thrills and snaps
in the same breeze that makes his nerves
fire, his bare lungs scream.
Stripped of himself and from his twin:
the stiffening scab and the sticky wound.

Marsyas the martyr, a god's fetish,
hangs from the tree like bad fruit.

Aberdeen

The grey sea turns in its sleep
disturbing seagulls from the green rock.

We watched the long collapse, the black drop
and frothing of the toppled wave; looked out
on the dark that goes to Norway.

We lay all night in an open boat, that rocked
by the harbour wall – listening to the tyres creak
at the stone quay, trying to keep time –
till the night-fishers came in their arc, their lap
of light: the fat slap of waves, the water's
sway, the water mullioned with light.

The sifting rain, italic rain; the smirr
that drifted down for days; the sleet.
Your hair full of hail, as if sewn there.
In the damp sheets we left each other sea-gifts,
watermarks: long lost now in all these years
of the rip-tide's swell and trawl.

All night the feeding storm banked up
the streets and houses. In the morning
the sky was yellow, the frost ringing.

The grey sea turns in its sleep
disturbing seagulls from the green rock.

At Dusk

Walking through the woods
I saw these things:
a cat, lying, looking at me;
a red hut I could not enter;
the white grin of the snared fox;
the spider in a milk bottle,
cradling the swaddled fly,
rocking it to sleep;
a set of car keys, hanging from a tree;
a fire, still warm, and a bone
the length of my arm, my name
carved on it, mis-spelt.
The dog left me there,
and I went on myself.

Visiting my Grandfather

In a room as dark as his
you remembered colour, in amongst
brown bakelite, teak,
and felt for furnishing,
the black-out curtains from the war.
I saw the blue cuneiform of the crossword
looming under the magnifier
for my father to finish;
the slow valves of the radio
warming like coals
into English voices;
the rainbow spills, for his pipe,
in a beaker by the hearth.
And the fire, of course, when lit,
full of all the usual pictures:
caves, dragons, life.
But being children
we were out too far to feel the heat,
kicking our legs on the high chairs,
nursing our flat lemonade
and trying not to see our blurred ghosts
in the dresser's unsilvering glass.

Once a year, though, it was summer,
and in the great window
were the white yachts of Stonehaven,
the yellow yachts in the bay.
As if colour TV
had come to Scotland, all afternoon
we watched a testcard
of acid primaries

on wavelengths of green
and a lemony blue.

It was a chill parlour, despite the fire,
but leaving was like opening
the door of a fridge: cold
dumping on your sandalled feet,
your bare legs.
Finding my way back from the kitchen,
arms out in the dark
for the connecting door,
I came against
a womanly thing,
some kind of shawl
or handbag dressed in feathers,
which I felt all over,
putting my hands down below –
till I touched the wetness,
neck and sudden beak,
left it swinging as I ran,
leaving half my life behind
with the hung pheasant
and half in my hands with its blood:
cinnabar, carnelian,
rose madder, rust.

Fireworks

'In the greatness of the flame he gave up the ghost'
                              Foxe's *Book of Martyrs*, XI

The poplars are emptied at dusk
like blown matches. A gust frees
and scatters the leaves in their last blaze:
the bronze husks catch and cartwheel
round and down the street to the park
in the smoke of a dark autumn,
from the thin, extinguished trees.

In the small lake, what had once been water
now was seamed with smoke,
marbled and macular,
dim and deep as wax,
with each stick and twig like a spilled wick
in the dulling hollow of the sconce:
metamorphosis in the cancelled pond.

By midnight the ice was dished, percussive,
blue-black under a bone moon.
Skipping stones on its steel deck
gave the sound of thrown springs,
railway lines, or fence-wire, singing.
I had scored a tracery of leaving, a map engraved,
a thrilling in the air.

After the park, the garden,
and the bright litter of the night's display:
a stubble of burnt-out cones and candles,
cold star-shells, burst and charred,
a catherine wheel fused to the bark;
scorched bottles, tapers; smoke, hanging;
the softening box on its bed of ash.

Hands cupped around a match's flame:
the blue twist of smoke. Petrol
is the fifth element: opening
a door in the night I can leave through.
Across the city, a scratch of light
disappears. I hear its stick
clattering in the trees.

Escapology

A shallow cut lets the blood bead:
and you could charm red bracelets,
coax necklaces from nowhere.
You stashed blades like savings,
pulled them out with a flourish
in a fan of silver.

Soon it was ribbons from the wrist
and sawing yourself in two; always
trying to disappear.
Then the finale: sedatives, restraints,
the escape-proof box. And you
lying there. A locked knife.

After the Overdose

What surprised me most?
Coming home to an open door,
rose petals everywhere, the bed
incongruous with blood?
The paramedic's satchel
left behind in all the rush?

Or you in the hospital,
the crusted corners of your mouth,
the gown they'd put you in?
You never wore short sleeves,
not since you burned a name
into your arm with cigarettes.

Or, finally, that you weren't dead?
That surprised me. That regret.

Lithium

After the arc of ECT
and the blunt concussion of pills,
they gave him lithium to cling to –
the psychiatrist's stone.
A metal that floats on water,
must be kept in kerosene,
can be drawn into wire.
(He who had jumped in the harbour,
burnt his hair off,
been caught hanging from the light.)
He'd heard it was once used
to make hydrogen bombs,
but now was a coolant for nuclear reactors,
so he broke out of hospital barefoot
and walked ten miles to meet me in the snow.

First Winter

Come and see this, I called,
this red bird at the feeder,
this striate sky,
these things I've done.

By the time you look you've missed it,
these lines are cold, the sky mussed,
the snow-shy cardinal
newly gone.

The Break

Washing glasses in the sink
and the first thing she knew was this
dull click, like a tongue,
under the soap-suds.
The foam pinked.
Now she could see blood
smoking from the flap of skin,
and it was over, clearly,
out in the open:
holding water, feeling nothing.

Raising the Paint

Pleased by the ruined bed,
the full ashtray,
I checked my glass for finger-marks:
turning it, over and over.
As I left the house
I ran the key
along the panels of the door,
raising the paint.
The tide was out,
and each step whitened the sand
like pressed skin.
Behind me, all this evidence:
an almost straight line
of footprints,
clothes, credit cards,
proving I exist.

Shot

You sleep as I stumble
room to room, unhelmed,
heavy-greaved;
coming to you
through gorse-light
and the fallen trees:
heraldic, blessed
with wounds.
Red-handed at the key
I was stock-still, gazing back
at deer-slots in the snow:
flushed, quick from the kill,
carrying my shot,
my sadness like a stone.
In the quarry-hole of your bed
you're sleeping still.

Jack-in-the-Green

Grinning soldiers
patrolling the border with biscuits,

tricked out in a motley of green and grey,
sooty faces, and leaves
where their hair should have been.

We came across one in the garden,
crouching: the Green Man abroad,
a compost of flesh and grass and metal,

haunched like a dog caught
shivering at its stool.

Hands of a Farmer in Co. Tyrone

He wore fish-gutter's gloves to pick brambles:
scoured leather, without fingertips,
so his fist could find the insides of the bush
and open around the soft black heart,
for the easing of the fruit.
He was a thorn in the fenced garden:
his hand at the command wire
paying out the line from culvert to sheugh.
They were on his land,
so he pulled the road up by the root.

Feeding the Fire

Some hard, half-eaten logs
lie drifting in ash:
black in the flocculent
smother of grey.
Just a puttering flame,
the occasional spat of cinder.

Holding a sheet of the *Times*
up against it, though,
the lung of paper sucked in
and suddenly lit from behind:
a roaring diorama;
the long throats of fire, feasting,

hungry for news. The page is read,
then reddened, then consumed.

Moving House

I. MIDDLE WATCH, BATTERSEA

Wash of traffic: the crush
of waves on a windowed shore;

the windows, worn to a shiver, let in rain.
The wind is posting litter through the door.

Behind the gas-fire in the hearth
a soot-fall clears the chimney's throat

and the wind sings wire-songs: the filament
blown like coal to a white gasp.

A scuffle in the skirting-board
as something frees itself from something else.

The bulb stirs and the room shifts
twice towards the cellar door.

II. DEFROSTING

The satisfying creak and give
of another white slab: ridged,
tectonic, holding the ice-box shape
in a curved mould; as if the polystyrene
once packed around the fridge
now packed inside, heavier and cold.
Small ice clatters in the salad drawer
as I hack at the top with a knife,
hands raw and hot in the sharp snow.
Bored, I take a warm beer through and write.
The fridge ticks with water, dripping;
the kitchen bobs towards me in the night.

Artichoke

The nubbed leaves
come away
in a tease of green, thinning
down to the membrane:
the quick, purpled,
beginnings of the male.

Then the slow hairs of the heart:
the choke that guards its trophy,
its vegetable goblet.
The meat of it lies, displayed,
up-ended, *al dente*,
the stub-root aching in its oil.

Blind Man Eating Winkles

Opening the door with a pin
he grubs for purchase,
tugging free
the firm twist of meat;
chewing it
as he roots out the next.

Specked with the rust-brown
circles, translucent as scabs,
he could sit here forever:
the rustle of the paper bag,
the shells scraping, the rummage
and shuck of the waves.

The Immoralist

In the sleeping ward, night-nurses
gather at my curtained bed,
looming like Rembrandts, drawing
their winged heads in around
the surgeon at my side.
The golden section lit by anglepoise:
the wrinkled fruit, some books,
my chest strapped like a girl's
to stem the leaking wound.

Scissoring the grey crêpe
released a clot dark as liver:
an African plum in its syrup
slid into my lap.
Jesus, I said, as the doctor called for swabs,
more light, the stitching trolley.
Without anaesthetics he worked quickly,
his pale hands deft
as a guitarist at the frets.
This is what they'd been waiting for:
one hand at the pliant flesh,
the other subduing it with suture
and a blurred knot.
Five minutes and it was over,
and he was smiling at the Gide
amongst the magazines and grapes:
Used to be just TB, this place, he said,
my blood on his cheek like a blush.

As the nurse drew back the curtain, she warned:
There will be pain.
Night flooded, streaming slowly into shape;
I heard the tinnitus of radio,
saw the humped figure under his lung of light,
the earphones' plastic stirrup on its hook,
his left hand in place on the white bandage
his right hand holding my book.

Silver Lake, Vermont

Familiar gestures in a fresh hand:
the lint and balsam,
sanctuary of the cooled flesh.
under a tissue moon, your hair untied,
your hair held back, the balm
of chrism dribbed against your side.

from **CAMERA OBSCURA**

Through the open door, and the latticed window,
light enters the dark room.

*

THE FLOWERS OF THE FOREST

Shouldering my daughter
like a set of pipes
I walk her
to a dead march
and counterpoint her crying
with my hummed drone:
the floo'ers o' the forest
are a' wi'ed awae

my cracked reed
blanking
on the high note,
the way a nib runs dry
in the rut it makes,
and splays.

*

CIRCUS ON CALTON HILL

Edinburgh burns below us,
this blazing day
where flame's invisible, a dark wave
lapping at the petrol's grain, as the fire-eaters
assuage their thirst.
The fanned embers of the city rustle
like the wrappers of sweets; heat
tinkering in the coal.
Sitting under the colonnade,
we are so close we almost touch.

Tumblers flip and flex,
desultory on the dry grass;
gulls channer in the stunned heat,
shedding air above us
and over the baking Craigleith stone,
to bank away to the airish Firth
and Inchkeith Island,
the Ferry and the May.
I watch you watching jugglers; the obligatory
lovers, and a snake-woman swallowing a sword.

You are turning heliotropic in this
acropolis of light, barely breaking sweat.
Lifting your hands to your hair a drop
runnels down under one arm to its cup
and the swell of your breast, and I am brimming,
scalding, kittling in the heat,
aching for you at the root of my tongue.
But I cannot find you; as you focus on the girl,
the girl on the grass below: her eyes closing,
her soft mouth as she bends to his.

*

FOUR VIEWS FROM THE CAMERA OBSCURA

A herringbone of pends and wynds,
tenements in a guddle on top of each other
with a common stair like a street on its end;
the stone cliffs of the city scarped
as steep as the trap rock;
the high *lands*, smoking hives.

In Princes Street Gardens
a grey man holds his daughter up to pee,
her dress up about her, and him shaking.
But he is not her father,
his trousers at his knees,
their Tennent's Lager spilling in the grass.

To the Old Waverley: through the giant Y and H
of its sign, through the net-curtain gap
to the room inside, a lobster-pot of macramé,
sweltry, gravid: the German video on
with the sound down: the threshing hotel bed,
abandoned drinks. The red mesh of scorpions.

You are in another country, I know, but I did
just see you on that corner, clearly,
then passing in that cab, head down,
dashing me a note perhaps. The sap of you
still on my hands. A trace.
Wait. Wait for me here.

*

Could I find your face, or mine,
in these mirrors? Could I bring you back
with this coherent light?

*

28 INVERLEITH ROW

Staring out at Arboretum,
I see one tree shudder, disengage,
and move out of frame,
resolving itself
into a spider.
I pull back from infinity
and find the glass fledged
with frost: a strung web
and a thin fish-bone
ferning every edge.

*

She put her hand on me,
the bud of her hand on mine,
and in my withering hands she died.

*

FLAGS OF AUTUMN

Thorn grows flat against the flank of Calton Hill,
wind grooming the close wall
has disinclined the snappers
in the tour-coach below; they stay inside.
The empty lanyards slap against the poles.

To the south, the castle, Arthur's Seat:
basalt wedges, door-stops
holding open history.
Skeins of the tour-guide's commentary
ravel past the rock
in snatches; the lone piper
tugs on a cigarette
and marches back to his car:
gonfalons of Gold Leaf
fray and separate behind.

To the north, the bright regalia
of the panel-beaten Firth.
A squall lifts the gorse
at the brink of the sea-fall:
the sky's film turned to fast-forward
as clouds bloom
like milk in water.
The rabbits scud and veer
through the flattening grass
and disappear with summer.

Put up like kites in the pulling rain, gulls
skirl their greeting over the stones.
And where we sat, stunned, that day,
those months ago: crows strut. Their black flags
flare and gutter in the gale.

*

FOUR VIEWS FROM THE CAMERA OBSCURA

The lens loses you in a blaze of traffic,
the murk of wynds; I track to the mouth
of Riddle's Court, to Lady Stair's Close,
but it clouds and I cannot find you. A clutch
of backpackers blocks my view, then the sun opens
and you are there. Your hair, your hand. A touch.

Driven through the wood's deep gully
the milling sheep were white water:
a shouldering slalom in the trees.
The river purls, its working muscle
turning in the tight glen below;
foam on its sides like a fleece.

Dawn: the harbour's curve
of stone – the shirr
of wind-flaw on water,
the falling of birds,
a woman waving
once from a window.

Both hands to her hair,
to the back of her head and the nape
of the neck, adjusting or unloosening
the warm braid in its simple knot;
the hair damp and heavy in her hands,
the root of each arm laid open and bare.

*

When I think of the womb of my daughter
– small as a thimble – I despair.

*   39

THE GIFT OF TANTALUS

After-images, the after-shocks of lives
lived here, still troubling the light.
As land consecrated by battle,
we return to places
where things happened
just to feel the air thrill,
know that what we came to find
is fading, leaching away,
while the place mocks us,
flashing up our mortality,
our young ghosts,
in a time-lapse film
of flowers and rotting fruit.
Dark replaces light, the trace
of happiness is grief.
We stand in our own spoor
listening for laughter,
hungry for a youth that's out of reach.

*

This lobster vanity draws me
to the mirror in the creel.

*

DUMB SHOW, WITH CANDLES

Still as a battlefield, the strewn city
goes under, slips into silhouette.
Some threads of smoke,
the lift and fall of flags in orange light.
The glinting windows go out one by one.

Low over the Firth, a fork of geese
comes pulling past, straight-necked:
creaking like rowlocks
over the frozen hill.
On the Parthenon below, querulous gulls
screel and skraik and peel away,
bickering, into the air's tow.
Too cold, even for them.
I circle the observatory one more time:
mine the only footprints in the snow.

Now the night has fallen, Edinburgh comes alight
as if each building's shell
has a fire inside that burned. The follies
– lit exhibits – stand here on the hill
in their white stone; the Castle glows.
And the streets are bright blurs of sodium
and pearl: the drawn tracery of headlamps
smeared in long exposure. For miles west
the city stretches,
laid with vapour trails and ghosts.

To the east, the folding sea has drowned
the girning of the gulls. A lighthouse
perforates the night: a slow cigarette.
Then there is no more light,
and no more breath or sound.

*

Desire becomes sorrow
just as night follows day
and today becomes tomorrow.

*

SUNNY MEMORIES

The year of the Sheep, the Year of Burning;
we shall return no more; the Rising,
from Glenfinnan to Culloden Moor;
potato famine; Nova Scotia;
Barra, Knoydart, Ardnamurchan.

Balmoral; the Sobieski Stuart Brothers'
Vestiarium Scoticum; clan maps and tartan,
Edinburgh rock; Walter Scott and Harry Lauder;
Wha's like us? Cheers! and *slàinte mhath*
to the king across the water.

*

I cannot always hold your hand
or cover your eyes,
my beautiful blue-veined daughter.

*

DEAD CENTRE, 1858

Exactly halfway through his life, panning east
on Princes Street, George Washington Wilson stopped
the moving world into focus. After long exposure,
ghosts returned to their bodies. Calton Hill rose
at the top of the frame, the grave-slots of the cemetery
a perfect *memento*. The first snapshot. Steady traffic.

*

EDINBURGH CASTLE (DETAIL)

The Japanese tourist
places his camera on a post,
backs away, and stands,
smiling vigorously.
The small machine flashes; clicks.
I hear the shutter's
granular slither
as a spade in wet soil,
while he would hear: *sha'shin*.

The whirr of winding-on.

He drops the smile,
picks up his Nikon and goes,
muttering about something,
punishing the ground.

*

FOUR VIEWS FROM THE CAMERA OBSCURA

In the Grassmarket, a girl in a red dress
steps between parked cars
into the forensic flash, flash of cameras.
Around her, the Pre-Raphaelite beauties
of Julia Margaret Cameron,
the mongols of Arbus.

Track east to the Calton
where Nelson's upturned telescope
stands staring at the ground,
where the observatory lies vacant, closed
a century ago by railway smoke
from Waverley: the Enlightenment below.

Gulls mill like ash around Valhalla,
over Calton Hill and the empty High School,
modelled on the Temple of Theseus,
the dark, echoing shell of independence.
The sooty Parthenon (unfinished) gapes down
on the black-sailed vessel anchored in the sound.

What I thought was a figure
standing in a doorway
was just a doorway;
the movement in the window
just a loss of light. Look:
my eyes are not my own.

*

With every step of hers towards the light
a step of mine towards the murk.

*

My daughter feels no fear
because of me.
I have it learnt
because of her.

*

THE ROYAL HIGH SCHOOL

After the children had gone
the gulls came in a white flit:
sentinel at windows,
falling between buildings.
The janitors and cleaners never saw them
dropping in: ambling down corridors,
looking into rooms, blinking
at their new estate.
They nest here now, among the jotters
and pencils, unopened boxes
of *The Scottish Constitution*;
living like kings
on a diet of silverfish,
long-life milk and chalk.

*

I look in the mirror and see nothing,
then turn to the window
and catch myself walking away.

45

AMNESTY IN THE GARDEN

A brim of light leaks out across the sea
to lift the bevel in the wave, the water's lens,
and everything moves again:
the pleated land renewed in its bloom
of gold, the broom and yellow gorse.
Gulls hang their hinges of light
over the loosened water, calling,
calling me down from the hill's height
and the high stones that remain,
what marks we made on them long effaced.

The forest creaks like a door.
Where children will come this morning
to make handsels for the May Queen
– gathering flowers of the forest
to draw the harvest of the sea –
a rabbit scutters in the leaf-litter,
squirrels shrug up trees, and a pheasant
clatters away like a mechanical toy.
Steeped again in the blent green,
A boy enters the walled garden.

A wind. The lilac and laburnum trees
seethe and churn, then settle. Above him,
the buds are swollen and opening;
below, red shoots spirl to the morning sun.
The roots swarm. In the walled garden
form is imposed on this fugitive green,
this rinsing light: to enclose is to make sacred,
to frame life's chaos for a slow repair,
to make an art of healing, of release,
an amnesty against despair.

*

46

Night breathes on me
and the world mists.
I make a window
in the mirror
for the face of my father,
tired of this.

*

Michael Hofmann

Touring Company

In your cavalier fashion, you leave your
small change on my floor. You keep pots of it
at home. – It feels sick to be alone again.
Like a charlady I shake my head at the dust,
and scrape it into pieces of knitting
with my fingers. – On the *Nautilus* there was
apparently never any dust, as all their air
came out of cylinders. But then Strindberg
or Hamsun, or another of those northern mis-
anthropes, writes that dust consists almost
entirely of dead human skin . . . Captain
Nemo's men can't have decomposed as we do.

Yesterday, you played five small male parts
in *Macbeth*: four cowards and a murdered child –
a friend drew a red line across your throat
with his dagger. I sat in the front row,
worrying about the psychological consequences
of being murdered every night for a month . . .
And the blood seeped into our private life;
that of the stars was washable, but yours was
permanent for economy. It pales on my sheets,
souvenir of your lovely blush . . . When you left,
you forgot your vanishing-cream – my biker,
spark-plugs mixing with tampons in your handbag!

First Night

Electrodes attached to a flautist's cheeks:
a measure of nerves, his fear of the performance.

You move the fifty-seven muscles it takes to smile.
It's strange to see you again. A faint tan

is like dust on your memory, a shade or two,
numbers along the spectrum of available paints . . .

A freshness about your eyes suggests you are
newly hatched, like Eve, in an unfamiliar world.

I cross my legs, and watch the twitch of reflex –
Plato's great longing, my foot helplessly kicking space.

Family Holidays

The car got a sun-tan while my father worked
in its compound . . . Mixed with the cicadas,
you could hear the fecundity of his typing
under the green corrugated plastic roof.

My mother staggered about like a nude
in her sun-hat, high heels and bathing-costume.
She was Quartermaster and Communications.

My doughy sisters baked on the stony beach,
swelling out of their bikinis, turning over
every half-hour. Still, they were never done.

The little one fraternized with foreign children.

. . . Every day I swam further out of my depth,
but always, miserably, crawled back to safety.

Boys' Own

(i.m. T. J. Park)

A parting slightly off-centre, like Oscar Wilde's,
his fat mouth, and the same bulky appearance.
Your hair was pomaded, an immaculate wet-look,
sculpted and old-fashioned in these blow-dry times.
The dull grain of wood on polished furniture.
– Everyone has an inspiring English teacher
somewhere behind them, and you were ours. We argued
about you: that your smell was not sweet after-shave,
but the presbyterian rigours of cold water –

on your porous face and soft, womanish hands . . . ?
The public-school teacher has to be versatile –
if not the genuine Renaissance article, then at least
a modern pentathlete – and so you appeared to us
in as many guises as an Action Man: for lessons,
with a gown over one of your heavy three-piece suits;
wearing khaki for Corps on Wednesday afternoons;
as a soccer referee in a diabolical black tracksuit;
in baggy but respectable corduroys on holidays . . .

Morning coffee was followed by pre-prandial sherry
after only the shortest of intervals. The empties,
screw-tops, stood in boxes outside your door.
You drank early, copiously, and every day –
though it hardly crossed our minds. Given the chance,
we would have done too . . . It was 'civilized',
and that was what you were about. Sweet and sour sherry,
lager on warm afternoons, the pathos of sparkling wine
for occasions. 'It's actually quite like champagne . . .'

Just as an extension-lead went from your gramophone
to its little brother, a 'stereophonic' loudspeaker –
Ferguson Major and Minor . . . With one hand in your
    pocket,
leaning back in your swivelling chair, you conducted
your own records, legs double-crossed like Joyce's.
– Among all those other self-perpetuating oddball
bachelors, how could we fail to understand you?
Your military discipline and vintage appearance,
the sublimation of your Anglicanism, your drinking . . .

We only waited for that moment at the end of a class,
when, exhausted by intellectual inquiry, you took off
your glasses and rubbed away your tiny blue eyes . . .
All of love and death can be found in books;
you would have agreed. At one of your gatherings,
someone found a pubic hair in your sheepskin rug . . .
Years later, there was a scandal, an ultimatum,
and you threw yourself under the wheels of a train –
the severe way Tolstoy chose for Anna Karenina.

Furth i. Wald

(for Jan and Anja T.)

There are seagulls inland, extensive flooding
and a grey sky. A tractor stalled in midfield
between two goals. Mammoth sawmills collecting trees
and pulping them for furniture and wallpaper . . .
These strips of towns, with their troubled histories,
they are lost in the woods like Hansel and Gretel.
Counters at peace conferences, they changed hands
so often, they became indistinguishable, worthless.
Polyglot and juggled like Belgium, each of them keeps
a spare name in the other language to fall back on.
Only their wanton, spawning frontier tells them apart,
an arrogant line of wire in an electric clearing.
(A modern derivative of the civic myth of Thebes:
the oxhide cut into ribbons by cunning estate agents,
and laid end to end; so many towns called Cuernavaca . . .)
– At other frontiers, it may be a long tunnel instead,
too long for you to hold your breath. At halfway,
the texture of the concrete changes, and the lights,
but you can't say where it is brighter or safer . . .
Nations are irregular parcels, tight with fear.
But their contents have settled during transport.
Grenzflucht. Perimeters that are now deserted and
timid, the dream-wrappings clash with each other.
On one side, the lonely heartless villas of the guards.
Dustbins stored like sandbags outside barrackrooms.
The play of searchlights . . . On the other, *Der Neue
Tag* dawns only twice a week nowadays. With its
Nazi-sounding name and millenarian ideals, still
holding the fort for a dwindling readership . . .

Nights in the Iron Hotel

Our beds are at a hospital distance.
I push them together. Straw matting
on the walls produces a Palm Beach effect:

long drinks made with rum in tropical bars.
The position of mirror and wardrobe
recalls a room I once lived in happily.

Our feelings are shorter and faster now.
You confess a new infidelity. This time,
a trombone player. His tender mercies . . .

All night, we talk about separating.
The radio wakes us with its muzak.
In a sinister way, you call it lulling.

We are fascinated by our own anaesthesia,
our inability to function. Sex is a luxury,
an export of healthy physical economies.

The TV stays switched on all the time.
Dizzying socialist realism for the drunks.
A gymnast swings like a hooked fish.

Prague

Body Heat

This evening belongs to a warmer day –
separated clouds, birds, bits of green . . .
We wake late, naked, stuck to each other:
the greenhouse effect of windows and bedclothes.

Fifty years late, you finish *Love on the Dole*.
– Who knows, perhaps it can really be done?
The Boots hair setting-gel no longer works;
your pecker is down. The underdog's leather jacket

is here to stay, the stubborn lower lip
of the disconsolate punk . . . The poor hedgehogs,
they must help each other to pull off the leaves
that covered them while they were hibernating.

Ancient Evenings

(for A.)

My friends hunted in packs, had themselves photographed
under hoardings that said 'Tender Vegetables'
or 'Big Chunks', but I had you – my Antonia!
Not for long, nor for a long time now . . .

Later, your jeans faded more completely,
and the hole in them wore to a furred square,
as it had to, but I remember my hands
skating over them, there where the cloth was thickest.

You were so quiet, it seemed like an invitation
to be disturbed, like Archimedes and the soldier,
like me, like the water displaced from my kettle
when I heated tins of viscous celery soup in it

until the glue dissolved and the labels crumbled
and the turbid, overheated water turned into more soup . . .
I was overheated, too. I could not trust my judgement.
The coffee I made in the dark was eight times too strong.

My humour was gravity, so I sat us both in an armchair
and toppled over backwards. I must have hoped
the experience of danger would cement our relationship.
Nothing was broken, and we made surprisingly little noise.

On the Margins

Hospitality and unease, weekend guests
in this Chekhovian rectory painted a frivolous
blush pink. It is comfortable and fallen,
as though run by children, but with an adult's
guiding hand for basics, food, warmth, light . . .
At other times, what conversations, what demeanours!
I stare at myself in the grey, oxidized mirror
over the fireplace, godless, inept, countrified.
The distance disappears between rooms and voices.
Stuffy and centripetal, I tag after my hosts,
talking, offering 'help', sitting on tables
or leaning ungraciously in the doorway.

We drove twenty miles to buy roses, to a stately home
behind a moat and a pair of netted Alsatians.
The shaggy, youthful master of the house
was already on to his second family. His little boy
must have guessed. He had the exemplary energy
of the late child, working on his parents' stamina,
boisterous and surexcited, running to fetch us
prayer books, one at a time, they were so heavy.

Back here, I feel again spiritless, unhappy, the wrong age.
Not to be condescended to, still less fit for equality.
I quarrel with you over your word 'accomplished',
and then slink off upstairs to make it up . . .
We hear the hoarse, see-saw cries of the donkeys
grazing in the churchyard, mother and daughter,
and the first mosquitoes bouncing up and down,
practising their verticals like a video game. Next door,
his green clothes hung on pegs, Eric, the rustic burr,
is taking a bath, whistling and crooning happily
in his timeless, folkloric voice. I pat your nakedness.
In evil whispers, I manage to convince you.

Changes

Birds singing in the rain, in the dawn chorus,
on power lines. Birds knocking on the lawn,
and poor mistaken worms answering them . . .

They take no thought for the morrow, not like you
in your new job. – It paid for my flowers, now
already stricken in years. The stiff cornflowers

bleach, their blue rinse grows out. The marigolds
develop a stoop and go bald, orange clowns,
straw polls, their petals coming out in fistfuls . . .

Hard to take you in your new professional pride –
a salary, place of work, colleagues, corporate spirit –
your new *femme d'affaires* haircut, hard as nails.

Say I must be repressive, afraid of castration,
loving the quest better than its fulfilment.
– What became of you, bright sparrow, featherhead?

A Floating City

'Un seul être vous manque, et tout est dépeuplé
                                    – Lamartine

After the card-players, the cuba libre drinkers
and the readers of two-day-old newspapers,
there are the night strollers, pastel shades down the
      bobble-lit
Atlantic esplanade, by the small roar of the waves.

We saw the passenger liner put in for the afternoon,
then put out again: a floating city, heading South,
then pulling a slow turn, end on to the shore,
and backing North-West for the Azores or the
      shipping-lanes –

a wide and wasteful curve, elegiac and deceptive,
like that of your plane (and its decoy), that I followed
standing in the jetstream as they lifted away,
penny-pinching Britannias on their chartered tails . . .

The place was demolished in an earthquake and rebuilt
on a new site: built down, having learned its lesson,
wide and flat, built for cars. – With you gone out of it,
it seems destroyed again, and rebuilt to less purpose.

I stand on Avenue Mohammed V like a crowd hoping for
      a motorcade.
When the King comes to stay, he's like an earthquake,
living with the one thing his paranoia can live with,
the migrant population he calls an entourage.

A Brief Occupation

(for Gilles Ortlieb)

Six floors up, I found myself like a suicide –
one night, the last thing in a bare room . . .
I was afraid I might frighten my neighbours,
two old ladies dying of terror, thinking
every man was the gasman, every gasman a killer . . .

I was not myself. I was just anyone. The next day,
the place was going to be sold. Every so often,
high-spirited car horns bypassed the dead-end street.
The outside wall was a slowly declining roof,
an electricity meter clung to life by a few threads . . .

There was an inhuman shortage of cloth in that room:
a crocheted rug with a few eloquent hairs on it,
a stone for a pillow, my coat hanging demurely in the
    window.
The hairs belonged to a girl, now back in Greece,
an island, a museum of mankind.

Nighthawks

(for James Lasdun)

Time isn't money, at our age, it's water.
You couldn't say we cupped our hands very tightly . . .
We missed the second-last train, and find ourselves
at the station with half an hour to kill.

The derelicts queue twice round the tearoom.
Outside, the controlled prostitutes move smoothly
through the shoals of men laughing off their fear.
The street-lamps are a dull coral, snakes' heads.

Earlier, I watched a couple over your shoulder.
She was thin, bone-chested, dressed in black lace,
her best feature vines of hair. Blatant, ravenous,
post-coital, they greased their fingers as they ate.

I met a dim acquaintance, a man with the manner
of a laughing-gas victim, rich, frightened and jovial.
Why doesn't everyone wear pink, he squeaked.
Only a couple of blocks are safe in his world.

Now we've arrived at this hamburger heaven,
a bright hole walled with mirrors where our faces show
pale and evacuated in the neon. We spoon our sundaes
from a metal dish. The chopped nuts are poison.

We've been six straight hours together, my friend,
sitting in a shroud of earnestness and misgiving.
Swarthy, big-lipped, suffering, tubercular,
your hollow darkness survives even in this place . . .

The branch-line is under the axe, but it still runs,
rattling and screeching, between the hospital
lit like a toy, and the castellated factory –
a *folie de grandeur* of late capitalism.

From Kensal Rise to Heaven

Old Labour slogans, *Venceremos*, dates for demonstrations
like passed deadlines – they must be disappointed
to find they still exist. Halfway down the street,
a sign struggles to its feet and says Brent.

The surfaces are friable, broken and dirty, a skin unsuitable
for chemical treatment. Building, repair and demolition
go on simultaneously, indistinguishably. Change and decay.
– When change is arrested, what do you get?

The Sun, our Chinese takeaway, is being repainted.
I see an orange topcoat calls for a pink undercoat.
A Chinese calendar girl, naked, chaste and varnished,
simpers behind potplants like a jungle dawn.

Joy, local, it says in the phone-booth, with a number
next to it. Or *Petra*. Or *Out of Order*, and an arrow.
This last gives you pause, ten minutes, several weeks . . .
Delay deters the opportunist as much as doubt.

In an elementary deception, the name of the street
is taken from a country town, and when I get up
I find my education is back to haunt me: Dickens House,
Blake Court, Austen House, thirteen-storey giants.

Some Sunday mornings, blood trails down the street
from the night before. Stabbing, punch-up or nosebleed,
it's impossible to know, but the drops fell thickly and easily
on the paving-stones, too many for the rules of hopscotch.

The roadway itself is reddish, the faded spongy brick
of the terrace is overpowered by the paintwork's
sweet dessert colours. They spoil it, but you understand
they are there as the sugar in tomato soup is there.

Clouds come over from the West, as always in England
the feeling that the sea is just beyond the next horizon:
a thick, Byzantine crucifix on a steep schoolhouse roof,
the slippery, ecclesiastical gleam of wet slate.

Dogs vet the garbage before the refuse collectors.
Brazen starlings and pigeons, 'flying rats', go over
what is left. Rough-necked, microcephalous, they have
too much white on their bodies, like calcium defectives.

The pigeons mate in full view: some preliminary billing,
then the male flutters his wings as though to break a fall . . .
They inhabit a ruined chiropodist's, coming and going freely
through broken windows into their cosy excremental hollow.

The old man in the vest in the old people's home
would willingly watch us all day. In their windows,
a kind of alcove, they keep wine bottles and candlesticks,
Torvill and Dean, a special occasion on ice.

The motor-mews has flat roofs of sandpaper or tarpaper.
One is terraced, like three descending trays of gravel.
Their skylights are angled towards the red East,
some are truncated pyramids, others whole glazed shacks.

Open House

Rawlplugs and polyfilla . . . the cheerful,
tamping thump of reggae through the floorboards,

the drawling vowel 'r' of Irish or Jamaican English
carrying easily through the heated, excitable air –

as though I lived in a museum without walls.

Between Bed and Wastepaper Basket

There hasn't been much to cheer about in three years
in this boxroom shaped like a loaf of bread,
the flimsy partitions of the servants' quarters,
high up in the drafty cranium of the house.

All things tend towards the yellow of unlove,
the tawny, moulting carpet where I am commemorated
by tea- and coffee-stains, by the round holes of furniture –
too much of it, and too long in the same place.

Here, we have been prepared for whatever comes next.
The dishonest, middle-aged anorexic has been moved on.
The radio-buff is now responsible for contact
in the cardboard huts of the British Antarctic Survey.

(His great antenna was demolished here one stormy night.)
The tiny American professor is looking for tenure.
On occasional passionate weekends, the vinegary
smell of cruel spermicide carried all before it.

Familiarity breeds mostly the fear of its loss.
In winter, the ice-flowers on the inside of the window
and the singing of the loose tap; in summer,
the thunderflies that came in and died on my books

like bits of misplaced newsprint . . . I seize the day
when you visited me here – the child's world in person:
gold shoes, grass skirt, sky blouse and tinted, cirrus hair.
We went outside. Everything in the garden was rosy.

Prefabs ran down the back of the Applied Psychology Unit.
Pigeons dilated. The flies were drowsy from eating
the water-lilies on the pond. A snake had taken care of
the frogs. Fuchsias pointed their toes like ballerinas.

My hand tried to cup your breast. You were jail-bait,
proposing a miraculous career as county wife
and parole officer. We failed to betray
whatever trust was placed in us.

Day of Reckoning

When we drove across America, going West,
I tanned through the sandwich glass windscreen.
Though I was eight, and my legs weren't yet long
in their long pants, I could still sit in front –

your co-driver who couldn't spell you . . .
My jagged elbow stuck out the right-hand window,
I kept a tough diary, owned a blunt knife,
and my mother sat in the back with the girls.

I can't remember if we talked, or if, even then,
you played the radio, but when I got tired
I huddled in my legroom in the Chevy Belair,
and watched the coloured stars under the dashboard . . .

I learned fractions from you in a single day,
multiplying and dividing. In Kingston, Ontario,
I had a cruel haircut. For you, it was a dry time –
in two years one short play about bankruptcy:

Let Them Down, Gently. There followed the great crash.

The Machine That Cried

'Il n'y a pas de détail'
          – Paul Valéry

When I learned that my parents were returning
to Germany, and that I was to be jettisoned,
I gave a sudden lurch into infancy and Englishness.
Carpets again loomed large in my world: I sought out
their fabric and warmth, where there was nowhere to fall . . .

I took up jigsaw puzzles, read mystical cricket thrillers
passing all understanding, even collected toy soldiers
and killed them with matchsticks fired from the World War
    One
field-guns I bought from Peter Oborn down the road
– he must have had something German, with that name –

who lived alone with his mother, like a man . . .
My classmates were equipped with sexual insults
for the foaming lace of the English women playing
    Wimbledon,
but I watched them blandly on our rented set
behind drawn curtains, without ever getting the point.

My building-projects were as ambitious as the Tower of
    Babel.
Something automotive of my construction limped across
    the floor
to no purpose, only lugging its heavy battery.
Was there perhaps some future for Christiaan Barnard,
or the electric car, a milk-float groaning like a sacred heart?

I imagined Moog as von Moog, a mad German scientist.
His synthesizer was supposed to be the last word in
    versatility,
but when I first heard it on Chicory Tip's
Son of my Father, it was just a unisono metallic drone,
five notes, as inhibited and pleonastic as the title.

My father bought a gramophone, a black box,
and played late Beethoven on it, which my mother was
    always
to associate with her miscarriage of that year.
I was forever carrying it up to my room,
and quietly playing through my infant collection of singles,

Led Zeppelin, The Tremoloes, *My Sweet Lord* . . .
The drums cut like a scalpel across the other instruments.
Sometimes the turntable rotated slowly, then everything
went flat, and I thought how with a little more care
it could have been all right. There again, so many things

were undependable . . . My first-ever British accent wavered
between Pakistani and Welsh. I called *Bruce's* record shop
just for someone to talk to. He said, 'Certainly, Madam.'
Weeks later, it was 'Yes sir, you can bring your children.'
It seemed I had engineered my own birth in the new
    country.

My Father's House Has Many Mansions

Who could have said we belonged together,
my father and my self, out walking, our hands held
behind our backs in the way Goethe recommended?

Our heavy glances tipped us forward – the future,
a wedge of pavement with our shoes in it . . .
In your case, beige, stacked, echoing clogs;

and mine, the internationally scruffy tennis shoes –
seen but not heard – of the protest movement.
My mother shook her head at us from the window.

I was taller and faster but more considerate:
tense, overgrown, there on sufferance, I slowed down
and stooped for you. I wanted to share your life.

Live with you in your half-house in Ljubljana,
your second address: talk and read books;
meet your girl-friends, short-haired, dark, oral;

go shopping with cheap red money in the supermarket;
share the ants in the kitchen, the unfurnished rooms,
the fallible winter plumbing. Family was abasement

and obligation . . . The three steps to your door
were three steps to heaven. But there were only visits.
At a party for your students – my initiation! –

I ceremoniously downed a leather glass of *slivovica*.
But then nothing. I wanted your mixture of resentment
and pride in me expanded to the offer of equality.

Is the destination of paternity only advice . . . ?
In their ecstasy of growth, the bushes along the drive
scratch your bodywork, dislocate your wing-mirror.

Every year, the heraldic plum-tree in your garden
surprises you with its small, rotten fruit.

Author, Author

'verba volant, scripta manent'

Can this be all that remains — two or three weeks a year,
sitting at the opposite end of the dinner table from my father?

To listen to his breathing, more snorting than breathing,
puffing out air through his nose during mouthfuls,

chewing loudly with open mouth, without enjoyment,
uninhibited, inhibiting, his only talk, talk of food?

And to watch myself watching him, fastidious and disloyal,
feeling my muscles through my shirt — an open knife!

(My own part of the conversation, thin, witty, inaudible,
as though I'd spoken in asides for twenty-five years.)

To come back to him unannounced, at regular intervals,
one of two or three unselfsufficient, cryptic,

grown-up strangers he has fathered, and see again
his small silver mouth in his great grizzled face,

head and stomach grown to childlike proportions,
supported on his unchanging, teenager's legs . . .

To come upon by chance, while emptying the dustbin,
the ripped, glittery foil-wrapping of his heart-medicines,

multiplication times-tables of empty capsules,
dosages like police ammunition in a civil disturbance,

bought for cash over the counter and taken according to
  need —
like his sudden peremptory thirst for a quart of milk.

If sex is nostalgia for sex, and food nostalgia for food,
his can't be – what did a child of the War get to eat

that he would want to go on eating, and to share?
Standing in the road as the American trucks rolled by:

chewing-gum, cigarettes, canned herrings, a kick in the teeth.
(The way it is with dogs, and their first puppy nourishment:

potato-peelings, or my maternal grandmother in East
    Germany,
and Chéri, her gay dog – pampered, shy, neurotic Chéri,

corrupted by affection, his anal glands spoiling with
    virginity –
she feeds him heart and rice, the only cooking she ever
    does.) . . .

After the age of fifty, a sudden flowering, half a dozen
    novels
in as many years – dialogue by other means: his main
    characters

maniacs, compulsive, virtuoso talkers, talkers for dear life,
talkers in soliloquies, notebooks, tape-recordings, last
    wills . . .

Hear him on the telephone, an overloud, forced bonhomie,
standing feet crossed, and one punishing the other for lying,

woken up once at midnight by a drunken critic
with his girl-friend hanging on the extension –

her sweet name not a name at all, but a blandishment –
finishing with promises, and his vestigial phrase of English

after ten years in England, '*Bye, bye.*' Then going off to pee,
like the boys at my boarding-school after fire-practice . . .

Till that time, I had a worshipful proximity with him,
companionable and idolatrous. If my nose wasn't hooked,

my hair not black and straight, my frame too long,
my fingers not squat and powerful, fitting the typewriter
   keys,

then it was my mother's fault, her dilution, her adulteration.
Home from England, I landed on a checkered pattern

of unwillingness and miserable advice. Not to take drugs,
not to treat my face with vinegar or lemon-juice,

to make influential friends, and not to consort with others.
And, on interesting subjects, either a silence

or the interviewee's too-rapid turning to his own
   experience . . .
Perplexed, wounded, without confidence, I left him to
   himself,

first going round the block on a small-wheeled bicycle
in one of his leather jackets, like an elderly terror;

or, now, on walks with my mother in the shitty park
among the burghers: his duffle-coat in the zoo of democracy.

A performance, like everything else . . . What's the point?
He wants only his car and his typewriter and his Magic
   Marker.

Every action he divides into small stages, every traffic light
on the way home, and each one he punctuates with a
   crucified 'So.'

I ask myself what sort of consummation is available?
Fight; talk literature and politics; get drunk together?

Kiss him goodnight, as though half my life had never
   happened?

Fine Adjustments

By now, it is almost my father's arm,
a man's arm, that lifts the cigarettes to my mouth
numbed by smoke and raw onions and chocolate milk.

I need calm, something to tranquillize me
after the sudden storm between us that left me shaking,
and with sticky palms . . . It only happens here,

where I blurt in German, dissatisfied and unproficient
amid the material exhilaration of abstract furniture,
a new car on the Autobahn, electric pylons walking

through the erasures in the Bayrischer Wald . . .
Once before, I left some lines of Joseph Roth
bleeding on your desk: '*I had no father – that is,*

I never knew my father – but Zipper had one.
That made my friend seem quite privileged,
as though he had a parrot or a St Bernard.'

All at once, my nature as a child hits me.
I was a moving particle, like the skidding lights
in a film-still. Provoking and of no account,

I kept up a constant rearguard action, jibing,
commenting, sermonizing. 'Why did God give me a voice,'
I asked, 'if you always keep the radio on?'

It was a fugitive childhood. Aged four, I was chased
round and round the table by my father, who fell
and broke his arm he was going to raise against me.

The Late Richard Dadd, 1817–1886

The *Kentish Independent* of 1843
carried his pictures of his father, himself
and the scene of his crime. The first photojournalist:
fairy-painter, father-slayer, poor, bad, mad Richard Dadd.

His extended Grand Tour took in the Holy Land
and ended in Bethlem Hospital, with its long panoptical
galleries, spider plants, whippets and double gaslights.
He had outlived himself at twenty-six . . .

There was one day he seemed to catch sunstroke.
He fancied the black, scorched beard of a sheik
would furnish him with some 'capital paintbrushes'.
Sailing up the Nile, on the *Hecate*,

they spent Christmas Day eating boiled eggs
and plum pudding, and playing cards for the captain's soul.
The temples at Luxor stood under a full moon, lightly
    boiled.
Sir Thomas got off to try and bag a crocodile.

The route up from Marseille went as the crow flies –
precipitately, a dash from ear to ear.
A fellow traveller let him play with his collar and tie,
until he pulled out 'an excellent English razor'.

There was his watercolour, *Dead Camel*,
and a series of drawings of his friends,
all with their throats cut,
Frith, Egg, Dadd, Phillip and O'Neill.

He saw himself as a catspaw, Osiris's right-hand man
on earth. His digs in Newman Street
contained three hundred eggs, and the earth
cracked when he walked on it.

Marvin Gaye

He added the final 'e'
to counteract the imputation of homosexuality.
His father was plain Revd Gay, his son Marvin III.

He slept with his first hooker
in the army, coming off saltpetre.
He thought there was another word for 'virgin' that wasn't
    'eunuch'.

Including duets, he had fifty-five chart entries.
His life followed the rhythm of albums and tours.
He had a 'couple of periods of longevity with a woman'.

He preached sex to the cream suits,
the halter tops and the drug-induced personality disorders.
When his hair receded, he grew a woolly hat and beard.

Success was the mother of eccentricity and withdrawal.
In Ostend he felt the eyes of the Belgians on him,
in Topanga someone cut the throats of his two Great Danes.

At forty-four, back in his parents' house,
any one of a number of Marvins might come downstairs.
A dog collar shot a purple dressing-gown, twice.

Freebird

'One forms not the faintest inward attachment, especially here in America.'
                                                                        – D. H. Lawrence

Six girls round the pool in Stranglers' weather,
tanning; then three; then one (my favourite!),
every so often misting herself
or taking a drink of ice water from a plastic beaker.

Only the pool shark ever swam
humming, vacuuming debris, cleverly avoiding its tail.
The white undersides of the mockingbirds
flashed green when they flew over.

The setting was a blue by pink downtown development,
Southern hurricane architecture in matchwood:
live-oaks and love-seats, handymen and squirrels,
an electric grille and a siege mentality.

The soil was cedar chips, sprinkler heads and ants.
A few transplanted azaleas with difficulty flowered.
On watering days,
the air stank of artesian sulphur.

I was cuntstruck and fat. My tight chinos
came from a Second Avenue surplus store
that had an RPG dangling from the ceiling.
Grenada had been; the campus killings came later.

I lived in three bare rooms and a walk-in refrigerator.
The telephone kept ringing for Furniture World.
I looked at the dirty waves
breaking on the blue carpet and said not exactly.

A con-artist called Washington showed me Greek letters
carved in his huge upper arm, and the pest control man,
his cry of a soul in pain, switched
the clicking roach boxes under the sink.

The frat boy overhead gave it to his sorority girl
    steamhammer-style.
Someone turned up the Lynyrd Skynyrd,
the number with the seven-minute instrumental coda.
Her little screams petered out, *inachevée*.

Up in the Air

The sky was breaking, and I felt little less numb
than the alcoholic devotedly spooning
pâté from a tub; than the divorcee's station wagon
with its dog-haired sheepskin dogseat;
or the birds barking in the trees to greet the day . . .

There was a grey heron standing on a green bank.
'Soul survivors' spilled out of the *Titanic*
in their once-fluorescent sailing whites.
You only live once. The record sang 'My Girl',
but that was a lie. She only shucked my cigarette packet,

as she danced before my eyes like the alphabet,
mostly like the letter A . . . I was Ajax,
I had stolen another man's captive, slaughtered sheep
like a maniac, counted my friends till
I fell asleep, now I would have to swim for it

in the greasy, yellow, woollen waves . . .
The bass drum went like a heart, there was a pillow
curled in the bottom of it for anchorage.
Our finger-joints shook in the free air,
sheep's knuckle-bones dicing for the seamless garment.

Three hours flat out on the hotel candlewick,
blunting my creases, then off to the airport
with its complement of tiny, specialized, ministering
vehicles. I sat over the wing, riveted, wary,
remembering ring fingers and flying kites.

Wheels

Even the piss-artist, rocking back and forth
on the balls of his feet like a musical policeman,
is making an irreversible commitment . . . He shivers.

(The faith, applications and know-how it takes
to do anything, even under controlled circumstances!)
I find in myself this absurd purposefulness;

walking through my house, I lean forward,
I lick my finger to open a door, to turn over a page,
or the page of a calendar, or an advent calendar.

It takes all day to read twenty pages,
and the day goes down in a blaze of television.
One blue day is much like another . . . The plane lands

with a mew of rubber and a few 'less-than' signs.
The ball, remembering who hit it, keeps going.
The choreographed car-chase is ruinously exciting,

but the wheels turn very slowly backwards,
to convince the viewer that, far from wasting time,
he's recreating himself. A Christmas Special!

From the great outdoors, there's the derision
of real cars, the honeyed drone of approachable taxis,
some man's immortal Jag, numbered DEB1T . . .

How it must cut past the huddle of water-blue Inyacars,
lining the elbow of the road: smashed imperatives,
wheelchair hulls, rhombuses, stalled quartz.

Schönlaterngasse

Better never than late like the modern concrete
firetrap firegaps spacing the Austrian baroque, *risi pisi*;
like the morgenstern lamp's flex leaking plastic links of gold,
leaving the cutglass nightlight good enough to drink;
like the same tulip reproduction twice in our hapless room,
where the twelve lines of a spider plant die without offshoot:
your period, which we both half-hoped wouldn't come.

From A to B and Back Again

The Northern Line had come out into the open,
was leaving tracks like a curving cicatrice.
There was Barnet, my glottal stop, trying hard
to live up to its name, colloquial and harmless and trite.

The place was sunny and congested, brick and green trim,
it had the one-of-everything-and-two-butchers
of a provincial town. First, I dropped into
the maternity hospital by accident . . .

The porter was an analphabete, but together
we found your name, down among the Os,
and there you were, my brave love,
in a loose hospital gown that covered nothing;

pale; on an empty drip; and eager to show me
your scars, a couple of tidy crosses
like grappling hooks, one in the metropolis,
the other some distance away, in the unconcerned suburbs.

Summer '87

I was lying out on the caesium lawn,
on the ribs and ligatures of a split deckchair,
under the Roman purple of a copper beech,
a misgrown fasces, all rods and no axe.

It was the double-zero summer, where the birds
stunned themselves on the picture windows
with no red bird cardboard cutout doubles to warn them,
where the puffball dandelion grew twice as high,

where it was better not to eat parsley.
Every Friday, the newspapers gave fresh readings,
and put Turkish hazelnuts on the index.
A becquerel might be a fish or a type of mushroom.

In Munich, cylindrical missile balloons
bounced table-high, head-high, caber-high, house-high.
The crowds on the Leopoldstrasse were thick as pebbles
on the beach. I lay out on the caesium lawn.

Las Casas

I leaned round the corner in a Gold Rush town –
fortunate, apprehensive and somewhat surprised to be there.
The wind was one hazard, and so were the ramps
and unevennesses on the pavements, and the streetsellers
with their *montóns* of oranges. The kerbs were high,
almost a foot, as though anticipating a flood or blizzard.
Everyone seemed to have come from somewhere else,
the gringos from Europe and North America, the Ladinos,
once, ditto, the Indians from their outlying villages.
Everyone was a source of money to everyone else.
Who had it: the pink- or blue-burned and -burnoused
Indians; the women, in their bosoms with their babies;
the kerchiefed figures bussed in on the back of *camións*;
the ugly, leggy, insouciant foreign girls;
or the Ladinos, of whom the Indians said
they were begotten by a Ladina and a dog
by the side of the road, 'the Ladina helping' . . . ?
It was a raw town. The shoe shops sold mincing machines,
hats and aluminium buckets shared a shelf, paper and iron
went together – for the staking of claims, perhaps?
A town of radio shops and funeral parlours –
the dead travelled to the aquamarine graveyard
in station wagons, horizontal, to music;
the living, upright, on pickups, also to music.
Of well-lit drink shops. Of illustrated marriage magazines
and spot-the-beachball shots in Kodak shops.
Of *Secrets of a Nunnery*, and two churches
facing each other on two hills, holding a lofty dialogue.
(One was a ruin.) Of patio-and-parapet housing,
and pastel shacks whose quick spread swallowed the airport.
Of unpaved streets, away from the centre.

Of everyone off the streets, paved or not, by eight o'clock.
Of the all-day screech of tortilla machines
and the scrape of rockets up the sky, a flash in the pan,
a percussive crash, a surprisingly durable cloud.
Jubilation, and no eyes raised.

Guanajuato Two Times

for Karl Miller

I could keep returning to the same few places
till I turned blue; till I turned into
José José
on the sleeve of his new record album,
'What is Love?';
wearing a pleasant frown and predistressed denims;
reading the double-page spread ('The Trouble with José José')
on his drink problem,
comparing his picture 'Before' and 'After' . . .
I could slowly become a ghost, slowly familiar,
slowly invisible, amiable, obtuse . . .
I could say 'Remember me?' to the blank bellhop,
and myself remember
the septet in the bandstand playing 'Winchester Cathedral',
and the clown coming in for coffee
and to count his takings and take off his face . . .
I could take on all my former beds for size.
Meander knowingly through twelve towns with twelve street
     names between them.
Sit on both sides of the municipal kissing seats,
shaking my head at the blanket men
and the hammock men, in their humorous desperation
offering me hammocks for four, for five, for six . . .
I could learn the Spanish for
'I shall have returned' or 'Hullo, it's me again!'
and get the hang of the double handshake,
first the palms, then the locked thumbs.
My dreams would moulder and swell and hang off me
like pawpaws. I could stand and sway like a palm,
or rooted like a campanile, crumbling slightly
each time the bells tolled, not real bells
but recordings of former bells, and never for me.

Michael Longley

Graffiti

It would be painful, tedious and late
To alter awkward monsters such as these
To charming princes — metamorphoses
That all good fairy tales accelerate —

One kiss and, in the twinkling of an eye,
The Calibans accepted, warts and all,
At long last resurrected from the sty,
So blond, so beautiful, and six feet tall.

Through billboard forests, mists of lingerie,
These track a princess unequipped to change
Herself or them: her hair no winds derange,
Her thighs are locked, her cleavage legendary.

Lips where large allure but no response is,
Her all too perfect body they endure
By pencilling these bouquets of moustaches
As love's own emblem, their own signature.

Despite an aura vast enough to toss
Her neon constellations through the land,
She, in a realm too fragile to withstand
A single hair that is superfluous,

In paper palaces lies wintering,
While these who decorate her lovely crotch
With pubic shrubbery and with a notch,
Unwittingly imply a sort of spring. —

Such passion thwarted, such artistry released!
O where would Beauty be without her Beast?

The Ornithological Section

in memory of John Harvey

Birds, such heavenly bric-à-bric
Without their guts, without their fears,
Despite the vital parts they lack
Have here maintained their proper cloth,
Have held their equilibrium
So perfectly, so many years,
Shed nothing but momentum,
Their only weather dust and moth.

Toward what feats and feasts they steer,
Toward what continents migrate,
Or simply why they disappear,
With feathers talons beaks and plumes
Kingfisher kestrel dodo swan
In life, in death can illustrate,
For ornithology keep on
Their uniforms, their best costumes.

In this unnatural treasury,
Though held thus by their own décors
And fixed in frozen augury,
Out of the past they dart and wade,
In such different skies to figure,
On so many half-remembered shores,
And are heading for the future,
By some deep need of ours conveyed.

Who quit their gay trajectories
Too suddenly, too long ago,
True to their movements, even these
Across our field of vision spill
And, while winging it through fable,

Fuse all we hope with what we know –
Their fate incontrovertible,
Their vanished bodies flying still.

We, with our histories left to spend,
Would have our actions thus defined
By that repose in which they end,
Would have these birds, these lively dead,
Who hesitate before they go
For ever out of sight and mind,
Whose long delays concern us so,
As our biographers instead.

We come as ornithologists –
As taxidermists we depart,
For here an urge we have persists
To recognize the tattered skins,
The bones come in at last to land
Of birds, entitled from the start,
Who take their places, make their stand
Where science ends and love begins.

Odyssey

Amateur witches and professional virgins,
Sirens and shepherdesses – all new areas
Of experience (I have been out of touch) –
Ladies, you are so many and various
You will have to put up with me, for your sins,
A stranger to your islands who knows too much.

Your coy advertisements for bed and breakfast
I take as read, if I feel inclined –
So easy-going am I through going steady
(Your photographs will never hang in my mind)
With one ear cocked for the weather forecast
I come ashore to you who remind me,

And, going out of my way to take a rest,
From sea sickness and the sea recuperate,
The sad fleets of capsized skulls behind me
And the wide garden they decorate.
Grant me anchorage as your paying guest –
Landladies, I have been too long at sea.

When I sight you playing ball on the sand,
A suggestion of hair under your arms,
Or, in shallows, wearing only the waves,
I unpack strictly avuncular charms –
To lose these sea legs I walk on land:
I linger till my boat fills up with leaves,

With snow or sunshine (whichever I prefer).
I see your islands as the residue
Of my sailor days, of this life afloat,
My lonely motive to abandon you,
Darlings, after each whirlwind love affair
Becalmed in logbook and in anecdote.

You have kept me going, despite delays –
On these devious shores where we coincide
I have never once outstayed my welcome
Though you all seem last resorts, my brides –
Your faces favourite landmarks always,
Your bodies comprising the long way home.

Words for Jazz Perhaps

for Solly Lipsitz

Elegy for Fats Waller

Lighting up, lest all our hearts should break,
His fiftieth cigarette of the day,
Happy with so many notes at his beck
And call, he sits there taking it away,
The maker of immaculate slapstick.

With music and with such precise rampage
Across the deserts of the blues a trail
He blazes, towards the one true mirage,
Enormous on a nimble-footed camel
And almost refusing to be his age.

He plays for hours on end and though there be
Oases one part water, two parts gin,
He tumbles past to reign, wise and thirsty,
At the still centre of his loud dominion –
THE SHOOK THE SHAKE THE SHEIKH OF ARABY.

Bud Freeman in Belfast

Fog horn and factory siren intercept
Each fragile hoarded-up refrain. What else
Is there to do but let those notes erupt

Until your fading last glissando settles
Among all other sounds – carefully wrapped
In the cotton wool from aspirin bottles?

To Bessie Smith

You bring from Chattanooga Tennessee
Your huge voice to the back of my mind
Where, like sea shells salvaged from the sea
As bright reminders of a few weeks' stay,
Some random notes are all I ever find.
I couldn't play your records every day.

I think of Tra-na-rossan, Inisheer,
Of Harris drenched by horizontal rain –
Those landscapes I must visit year by year.
I do not live with sounds so seasonal
Nor set up house for good. Your blues contain
Each longed-for holiday, each terminal.

To Bix Beiderbecke

In hotel rooms, in digs you went to school.
These dead were voices from the floor below
Who filled like an empty room your skull,

Who shared your perpetual one-night stand
– The havoc there, and the manœuvrings! –
Each coloured hero with his instrument.

You were bound with one original theme
To compose in your head your terminus,
Or to improvise with the best of them.

That parabola from blues to barrelhouse.

The Rope-makers

Sometimes you and I are like rope-makers
Twisting straw into a golden cable,
So gradual my walking backwards
You fail to notice when I reach the door,
Each step infinitesimal, a delay,
Neither a coming nor a going when
Across the lane-way I face you still
Or, at large at last in the sunny fields,
Struggle to pick you out of the darkness
Where, close to the dresser, the scrubbed table,
Fingers securing the other end, you
Watch me diminish in a square of light.

Irish Poetry

Impasto or washes as a rule:
Tuberous clottings, a muddy
Accumulation, internal rhyme –
Fuchsia's droop towards the ground,
The potato and its flower:

Or a continuing drizzle,
Specializations of light,
Bog-water stretched over sand
In small waves, elisions –
The dialects of silence:

Or, sometimes, in combination
Outlining the bent spines,
The angular limbs of creatures –
Lost minerals colouring
The initial letter, the stance.

Carrigskeewaun

for Penny and David Cabot

The Mountain

This is ravens' territory, skulls, bones,
The marrow of these boulders supervised
From the upper air: I stand alone here
And seem to gather children about me,
A collection of picnic things, my voice
Filling the district as I call their names.

The Path

With my first step I dislodge the mallards
Whose necks strain over the bog to where
Kittiwakes scrape the waves: then, the circle
Widening, lapwings, curlews, snipe until
I am left with only one swan to nudge
To the far side of its gradual disdain.

The Strand

I discover, remaindered from yesterday,
Cattle tracks, a sanderling's tiny trail,
The footprints of the children and my own
Linking the dunes to the water's edge,
Reducing to sand the dry shells, the toe-
And fingernail parings of the sea.

The Wall

I join all the men who have squatted here
This lichened side of the dry-stone wall
And notice how smoke from our turf fire
Recalls in the cool air above the lake
Steam from a kettle, a tablecloth and
A table she might have already set.

The Lake

Though it will duplicate at any time
The sheep and cattle that wander there,
For a few minutes every evening
Its surface seems tilted to receive
The sun perfectly, the mare and her foal,
The heron, all such special visitors.

Wounds

Here are two pictures from my father's head —
I have kept them like secrets until now:
First, the Ulster Division at the Somme
Going over the top with 'Fuck the Pope!'
'No Surrender!': a boy about to die,
Screaming 'Give 'em one for the Shankill!'
'Wilder than Gurkhas' were my father's words
Of admiration and bewilderment.
Next comes the London-Scottish padre
Resettling kilts with his swagger-stick,
With a stylish backhand and a prayer.
Over a landscape of dead buttocks
My father followed him for fifty years.
At last, a belated casualty,
He said — lead traces flaring till they hurt —
'I am dying for King and Country, slowly.'
I touched his hand, his thin head I touched.

Now, with military honours of a kind,
With his badges, his medals like rainbows,
His spinning compass, I bury beside him
Three teenage soldiers, bellies full of
Bullets and Irish beer, their flies undone.
A packet of Woodbines I throw in,
A lucifer, the Sacred Heart of Jesus
Paralysed as heavy guns put out
The night-light in a nursery for ever;
Also a bus-conductor's uniform —
He collapsed beside his carpet-slippers
Without a murmur, shot through the head
By a shivering boy who wandered in
Before they could turn the television down
Or tidy away the supper dishes.
To the children, to a bewildered wife,
I think 'Sorry Missus' was what he said.

Kindertotenlieder

There can be no songs for dead children
Near the crazy circle of explosions,
The splintering tangent of the ricochet,

No songs for the children who have become
My unrestricted tenants, fingerprints
Everywhere, teethmarks on this and that.

The Island

The one saddle and bit on the island
We set aside for every second Sunday
When the priest rides slowly up from the pier.
Afterwards his boat creaks into the mist.
Or he arrives here nine times out of ten
With the doctor. They will soon be friends.

Visitors are few. A Belgian for instance
Who has told us all about the oven,
Linguists occasionally, and sociologists.
A lapsed Capuchin monk who came to stay
Was first and last to fish the lake for eels.
His carved crucifixes are still on sale.

One ship continues to rust on the rocks.
We stripped it completely of wash-hand basins,
Toilet fitments, its cargo of linoleum
And have set up house in our own fashion.
We can estimate time by the shadow
Of a doorpost inching across the floor.

In the thatch blackbirds rummaging for worms
And our dead submerged beneath the dunes.
We count ourselves historians of sorts
And chronicle all such comings and goings.
We can walk in a day around the island.
We shall reach the horizon and disappear.

Weather

I carry indoors
Two circles of blue sky,
Splinters of sunlight
As spring water tilts
And my buckets, heavy

Under the pressure of
Enormous atmospheres,
Two lakes and the islands
Enlarging constantly,
Tug at my shoulders, or,

With a wet sky low as
The ceiling, I shelter
Landmarks, keep track of
Animals, all the birds
In a reduced outdoors

And open my windows,
The wings of dragonflies
Hung from an alder cone,
A raindrop enclosing
Brookweed's five petals.

The Lodger

The lodger is writing a novel.
We give him the run of the house
But he occupies my mind as well –
An attic, a lumber-room
For his typewriter, notebooks,
The slowly accumulating pages.

At the end of each four-fingered
Suffering line the angelus rings –
A hundred noons and sunsets
As we lie here whispering,
Careful not to curtail our lives
Or change the names he has given us.

The Goose

Remember the white goose in my arms,
A present still. I plucked the long
Flight-feathers, down from the breast,
Finest fuzz from underneath the wings.

I thought of you through the operation
And covered the unmolested head,
The pink eyes that had persisted in
An expression of disappointment.

It was right to hesitate before
I punctured the skin, made incisions
And broached with my reluctant fingers
The chill of its intestines, because

Surviving there, lodged in its tract,
Nudging the bruise of the orifice
Was the last egg. I delivered it
Like clean bone, a seamless cranium.

Much else followed which, for your sake,
I bundled away, burned on the fire
With the head, the feet, the perfect wings.
The goose was ready for the oven.

I would boil the egg for your breakfast,
Conserve for weeks the delicate fats
As in the old days. In the meantime
We dismantled it, limb by limb.

Ars Poetica

I

Because they are somewhere in the building
I'll get in touch with them, the wife and kids —
Or I'm probably a widower by now,
Divorced and here by choice, on holiday
And paying through the nose for it; a queue
Of one outside the bathroom for ever
And no windows with a view of the sea.

II

I am writing a poem at the office desk
Or else I am forging business letters —
What I am really up to, I suspect,
Is seducing the boss's secretary
Among the ashtrays on the boardroom table
Before absconding with the petty-cash box
And a one-way ticket to Katmandu.

III

I go disguised as myself, my own beard
Changed by this multitude of distortions
To stage whiskers, my hair a give-away,
A cheap wig, and my face a mask only —
So that, on entering the hall of mirrors
The judge will at once award the first prize
To me and to all of my characters.

IV

After I've flown my rickety bi-plane
Under the Arc de Triomphe and before
I perform a double back-somersault
Without the safety net and – if there's time –
Walk the high wire between two waterfalls,
I shall draw a perfect circle free-hand
And risk my life in a final gesture.

V

Someone keeps banging the side of my head
Who is well aware that it's his furore,
His fists and feet I most want to describe –
My silence to date neither invitation
Nor complaint, but a stammering attempt
Once and for all to get him down in words
And allow him to push an open door.

VI

I am on general release now, having
Put myself in the shoes of all husbands,
Dissipated my substance in the parlours
Of an entire generation and annexed
To my territory gardens, allotments
And the desire – even at this late stage –
To go along with the world and his wife.

Stilts

for Paul Muldoon

Two grandfathers sway on stilts
Past my bedroom window.
They should be mending holes
In the Big Top, but that would be
Like putting out the stars.

The first has been a teacher
Of ballroom dancing, but now
Abandons house and home
To lift in the Grand Parade
High knees above the neighbours.

The second, a carpenter,
Comes from another town
With tools and material
To manufacture stilts
And playthings for the soul.

Architecture

The House on the Seashore

Laying down sand and shingle for the floor
And thatching with seaweed the low boulders
You make an echo-chamber of your home
That magnifies the wind to a cyclone
And keeps you from standing head and shoulders
Above the sea's whisper and the seashore.

The House Shaped Like an Egg

Do you pay for this house with egg money
Since its whitewashed walls are clean as shell
And the parlour, scullery, bedrooms oval
To leave no corner for dust or devil
Or the double yolk of heaven and hell
Or days when it rains and turns out sunny?

The House on the Bleach Green

This stump of a tree without any leaves
Can be occupied but never lived in
When snow is lying on the bleach green
And the smallest house you have ever seen
Lets someone inside to watch the linen
From tiny windows with a view of thieves.

The House Made out of Turf

Are the hearth and the chimney built of stone
Or can there be a fireplace for the fire
In a house made out of turf, with its roof
Of kindling, gables that may waterproof
This spacious tinderbox to make a pyre
Of what you built and heated on your own?

Oliver Plunkett

His Soul

When they cut off his head, the long whiskers
Went on growing, as if to fledge his soul
And facilitate its gradual departure.

So much of him was concentrated there
That, quite without his realizing it,
They divided the body into four.

It amounted to more than a withdrawal
When the last drop of moisture had dispersed
And one by one the hairs fell from his chin,

For the fatty brain was shrivelling as well,
Leaving around itself enormous spaces
And accommodation for the likes of him.

His own leathery shrine, he seems to be
Refracting the gleam in his father's eye
Like a shattered mirror in a handbag.

His Head

This is the end of the body that thinks
And says things, says things as the body does –
Kisses, belches, sighs – while making room for
The words of wisdom and the testimonies.

And these are a baby's features, a child's
Expression condensing on the plate glass,
The specimen suspended in its bottle
At eye level between shelf and shelf.

His head looks out from the tiny coffin
As though his body were crouching there
Inside the altar, a magician
Who is in charge of this conjuring trick,

Or an astronaut trapped by his oxygen
And eager to float upwards to the ceiling
Away from the gravitational pull
Of his arms and legs which are very old.

Your own face is reflected by the casket
And this is anybody's head in a room
Except that the walls are all windows and
He has written his name over the glass.

His Body

Trying to estimate what height he was
Keeps the soul awake, like the pea under
The heap of mattresses under the princess.

And now that they've turned him into a saint
Even a fly buzzing about the roof space
Must affect the balance of his mind.

His thigh bones and shoulder blades are scales
That a speck of dust could tilt, making him
Walk with a limp or become a hunchback.

He has been buried under the fingernails
Of his executioners, until they too fade
Like the lightning flash of their instruments.

There accompanies him around the cathedral
Enough silence to register the noise
Of the hairs on arms and legs expiring.

On Hearing Irish Spoken

Gliding together in a tidal shimmer to talk
Two fishermen leave behind another currach
Upturned on the beach, a hand cupped to an ear,

An echo of technical terms, the one I know
Repeating itself at desperate intervals
Like the stepping stones across a river in spate.

from **MAYO MONOLOGUES**

ARREST

The sergeant called me by my christian name
And waited an hour while I tidied up.
Not once did he mention why he had come
Or when and where he would take me away.
He just moved quietly from wall to wall
As I swept the floor towards the flagstones
And leaned brush and shovel, the broken tongs
Next to the spade and hoe I'd brought inside.
I emptied the half-used packet of tea
Into the caddy and dusted the lid.
In the leaky basin with its brown ring
I washed knife, fork, spoon, the two teacups
And the saucer that does for an ashtray.
I put back the stools where they usually stand,
Hung the towel to dry over one of them
And spread fresh newspapers on the table.
When I'd thrown the water from the basin
I turned it upside down on the turf stack,
Then I packed my shaving brush and razor
And smoored the fire as though I might return.
They have locked me up in the institute
Because I made love to the animals.
I'd sooner stand barefoot, without a cap
And take in my acres from a distance,
From the rocky hilltops or the seashore,
From the purgatory of the windy gaps.

Mountain Swim

Hilltop and valley floor we sway between,
Our bodies sustained as by a hammock,
Our nakedness water stretched on stone,

One with the shepherd's distant whistle,
The hawk lifted on its thermal, the hare
Asleep in its excrement like a child.

Meniscus

You are made out of water mostly, spittle, tears
And the blood that colours your cheek, red water.
Even your ears are ripples, your knuckles, knees
Damp stones that wear the meniscus like a skin.
Your breasts condense and adhere, drops of water.
And, where your body curves like a basin, faces
Are reflected, then dissolved by swaying water.

Dead Men's Fingers

The second time we meet I am waiting in a pub
Beside the cigarette machine. She is in her moons.
A cat with a mouse's tail dangling out of its mouth
Flashes from between her legs and escapes into my head.
There follow trips to the seaside where I find for her
Feathers, shells, dune violets among the marram grass;

Then the conversational strolls in a forest of pines
So that I can picture the invisible tree-creeper
Spiralling up her body to probe for such parasites
As lurk where pink flowers seem to harden into cones.
Next comes that honeymoon weekend in a farflung cottage
Where we sit in silence and borrow light from the door,

And I boil a somnolent lobster in the ash bucket
And divide it between us. Our most memorable meal.
But surely she has eaten dead men's fingers by mistake
Because her sickness interrupts us like a telephone.
The tenth, eleventh, twelfth occasions melt together
Colourfully: a stained-glass window in a burning church.

Indeed, I soon find myself, wherever a fire is lit,
Crossing my legs, putting my feet up on the mantelpiece
And talking to my shoes, with glances in her direction.
The first time we meet is really the last time in reverse.
We kiss for ever and I feel like the ghost of a child
Visiting the mother who long ago aborted him.

Florence Nightingale

Through your pocket glass you have let disease expand
To remote continents of pain where you go far
With rustling cuff and starched apron, a soft hand:
Beneath the bandage maggots are stitching the scar.

For many of the men who lie there it is late
And you allow them at the edge of consciousness
The halo of your lamp, a brothel's fanlight
Or a nightlight carried in by nanny and nurse.

You know that even with officers and clergy
Moustachioed lips will purse into fundaments
And under sedation all the bad words emerge
To be rinsed in your head like the smell of wounds,

Death's vegetable sweetness at both rind and core –
Name a weed and you find it growing everywhere.

No Man's Land

in memory of Isaac Rosenberg

I

Who will give skin and bones to my Jewish granny?
She has come down to me in the copperplate writing
Of three certificates, a dog-eared daguerreotype
And the one story my grandfather told about her.

He tossed a brick through a rowdy neighbour's window
As she lay dying, and Jessica, her twenty years
And mislaid whereabouts gave way to a second wife,
A terrible century, a circle of christian names.

II

I tilt her head towards you, Isaac Rosenberg,
But you can pick out that echo of splintering glass
From under the bombardment, and in No Man's Land
What is there to talk about but difficult poems?

Because your body was not recovered either
I try to read the constellations of brass buttons,
Identity discs that catch the light a little.
A shell-shocked carrier pigeon flaps behind the lines.

The Third Light

The sexton is opening up the grave,
Lining with mossy cushions and couch grass
This shaft of light, entrance to the earth
Where I kneel to marry you again,
My elbows in darkness as I explore
From my draughty attic your last bedroom.
Then I vanish into the roof space.

I have handed over to him your pain
And your preference for Cyprus sherry,
Your spry quotations from the *Daily Mail*
With its crossword solved in ink, your limp
And pills, your scatter of cigarette butts
And last-minute humorous spring-cleaning
Of one corner of a shelf in his cupboard.

You spent his medals like a currency,
Always refusing the third light, afraid
Of the snipers who would extinguish it.
Waiting to scramble hand in hand with him
Out of the shell hole, did you imagine
A Woodbine passing to and fro, a face
That stabilizes like a smoke ring?

Halley's Comet

Homage to Erik Satie

It was the seventeenth variation after all.
The original theme had fluttered out of my hands
And upside down on the linoleum suggested it.
An ink blot on the stave inspired the modulation,
Or was it a bloodstain, a teardrop's immortality
Perfectly pitched between parallels, horizontals,
The provisional shorelines, amphibian swamps?
I got drunk on a pint mug full of white feathers.
I couldn't sleep because inside my left nostril
A hair kept buzzing with signals from Halley's comet
As it swung its skirt of heavenly dust particles
On a parabola around the electric light bulb.
This won't recur for another seventy-six years.

The Shack

for Dillon and Guinn

I lie awake between the two sleeping couples.
Their careful breathing in the Blue Ridge Mountains
Disturbs me more than the engine ticking over
At the end of the lane, the repetitive whippoorwill,
The downpour's crescendo on corrugated iron.
Though there are no doors between them and me, perhaps
They will risk making love like embarrassed parents
While I remain motionless on my creaking divan.
They have shown me a copperhead, indian fire pinks
And buzzards like mobiles where the storm clouds hang.
I might as well be outside in the steamy field
Interrupting again the opossums' courtship,
Paralysing with torchlight pink noses, naked tails
Just beyond the shithouse where, like a fall of snow,
The equalizing lime has covered our excrement.
Tomorrow when we pass the Pentecostal church
The wayside pulpit will read 'Thanks, Lord, for the rain.'

Ghetto

I

Because you will suffer soon and die, your choices
Are neither right nor wrong: a spoon will feed you,
A flannel keep you clean, a toothbrush bring you back
To your bathroom's view of chimney-pots and gardens.
With so little time for inventory or leavetaking,
You are packing now for the rest of your life
Photographs, medicines, a change of underwear, a book,
A candlestick, a loaf, sardines, needle and thread.
These are your heirlooms, perishables, worldly goods.
What you bring is the same as what you leave behind,
Your last belonging a list of your belongings.

II

As though it were against the law to sleep in pillows
They have filled a cathedral with confiscated feathers:
Silence irrefrangible, no room for angels' wings,
Tons of feathers suffocating cherubim and seraphim.

III

The little girl without a mother behaves like a mother
With her rag doll to whom she explains fear and anguish,
The meagreness of the bread ration, how to make it last,
How to get back to the doll's house and lift up the roof
And, before the flame-throwers and dynamiters destroy it,
How to rescue from their separate rooms love and sorrow,
Masterpieces the size of a postage stamp, small fortunes.

IV

From among the hundreds of thousands I can imagine one
Behind the barbed-wire fences as my train crosses Poland.
I see him for long enough to catch the sprinkle of
    snowflakes
On his hair and schoolbag, and then I am transported
Away from that world of broken hobby-horses and silent
    toys.
He turns into a little snowman and refuses to melt.

V

For street-singers in the marketplace, weavers, warp-makers,
Those who suffer in sewing-machine repair shops,
    excrement-
Removal workers, there are not enough root vegetables,
Beetroots, turnips, swedes, nor for the leather-stitchers
Who are boiling leather so that their children may eat;
Who are turning like a thick slice of potato-bread
This page, which is everything I know about potatoes,
My delivery of Irish Peace, Beauty of Hebron, Home
Guard, Arran Banners, Kerr's Pinks, resistant to eelworm,
Resignation, common scab, terror, frost, potato-blight.

VI

There will be performances in the waiting room, and time
To jump over a skipping rope, and time to adjust
As though for a dancing class the ribbons in your hair.
This string quartet is the most natural thing in the world.

VII

Fingers leave shadows on a violin, harmonics,
A blackbird fluttering between electrified fences.

VIII

Lessons were forbidden in that terrible school.
Punishable by death were reading and writing
And arithmetic, so that even the junior infants
Grew old and wise in lofts studying these subjects.
There were drawing lessons, and drawings of kitchens
And farms, farm animals, butterflies, mothers, fathers
Who survived in crayon until in pen and ink
They turned into guards at executions and funerals
Torturing and hanging even these stick figures.
There were drawings of barracks and latrines as well
And the only windows were the windows they drew.

Stone-in-Oxney

for George Newson

At a table which seems to take root in the lawn
We breakfast late to a single propeller's drone,
The ghost of a Spitfire over Stone-in-Oxney
Or a Stuka, its turning-circle that cloud-gap
Or wherever you point to show me a bird; its dive
Low as the ceiling-beams in Chapel Cottage.
We bump against pilots who hang out of the sky.
Someone's hand is overshadowing the place-names,
Tracking the migration of wheatears and blackcaps
Who cross the Channel and make their landfall here.
Let him spread his fingers on a broken wing, now
Reed warblers are singing at Wittersham Levels
And at Small Hythe and Peening Quarter nightingales.

Eurycleia

I

Eurycleia fetched a basin, poured cold water into it,
Added hot water, and got ready to wash his feet.
But Odysseus shifted out of the firelight, afraid
She might notice his scar, the key to his identity,
A wound a boar inflicted years back, a flesh-wound.
His wet-nurse cradled his foot in her hands and touched
The scar, and recognising him she let go of his leg
Which clattered into the basin – water everywhere,
Such pain and happiness, her eyes filling with tears,
Her old voice cracking as she stroked his beard and
    whispered
'You are my baby boy for sure and I didn't know you
Until I had fondled my master's body all over.'

II

I began like Odysseus by loving the wrong woman
Who has disappeared among the skyscrapers of New York
After wandering for thousands of years from Ithaca.
She alone remembers the coppice, dense and overgrown,
Where in a compost of dead leaves the boar conceals
Its bristling spine and fire-red eyes and white tusks.

Trade Winds

I

Through Molly Ward's and Mickey Taylor's Locks,
Through Edenderry, Aghalee and Cranagh
To Lough Neagh and back again went Perseverance
And Speedwell carrying turf, coal and cinders.

II

Was it an Armagh man who loaded the boat
With the names of apples for his girlfriend:
Strawberry Cheeks, Lily Fingers, Angel Bites,
Winter Glories, Black Annetts, Widows' Whelps?

III

For smoking at wakes and breaking on graves
Carrick men christened clay pipes in Pipe Lane
Keel Baltic, Swinyard Cutty, Punch Quelp,
Plain Home Rule, Dutch Straws, Bent Unique.

IV

Among the Portavogie prawn-fishermen
Which will be the ship of death: Trade Winds,
Guiding Starlight, Halcyon, Easter Morn,
Liberty, Faithful Promise, Sparkling Wave?

Sitting for Eddie

in memory of Edward McGuire

I had suggested a spray of beech leaves behind me
Or a frieze of birds – bittern, lapwing, chough –
Or a single carline-thistle representing flowers
Pressed between pages, stuffed birds behind glass, our
Still lives, Eddie's and mine, feathers and petals
That get into the picture like noises-off, long
Distance calls in the small hours, crazed arguments
About the colour of my eyes – his strange mistake –
Jazz to relax me, in an enormous magnifying
Glass our eyes out of all proportion, likenesses
And the trundle of castors under a skylight,
His gambler's eye-shield, the colours of the rainbow,
Me turning into a still life whose eyes are blue.

Perdix

In the wings of that story about the failure of wings
– Broken wings, wings melting, feathers on water, Icarus –
The garrulous partridge crows happily from a sheugh
And claps its wings, a hitherto unheard-of species,
The latest creation, a grim reminder to Daedalus
– Inventor, failure's father – of his apprentice, a boy
Who had as a twelve-year-old the mental capacity
To look at the backbone of a fish and invent the saw
By cutting teeth in a metal blade; to draw conclusions
And a circle with the first compass, two iron limbs,
Arms, legs tied together, geometry's elbow or knee –

Which proved his downfall, for Daedalus grew so jealous
He pushed the prodigy headlong off the Acropolis
And then fibbed about him slipping; but Pallas Athene
Who supports the ingenious, intercepted his fall,
Dressed him in feathers in mid-air and made him a bird,
Intelligence flashing to wing-tip and claw, his name
Passing on to the bird (it is *perdix* in the Greek) –
The partridge that avoids getting airborne and nesting
In tree-tops or on dizzy ledges; that flapping along
At ground level, laying its eggs under hedges, has lost,
Thanks to the memory of that tumble, its head for heights.

Spiderwoman

Arachne starts with Ovid and finishes with me.

Her hair falls out and the ears and nostrils disappear
From her contracting face, her body minuscule, thin
Fingers clinging to her sides by way of legs, the rest
All stomach, from which she manufactures gossamer
And so keeps up her former trade, weaver, spider

Enticing the eight eyes of my imagination
To make love on her lethal doily, to dangle sperm
Like teardrops from an eyelash, massage it into her
While I avoid the spinnerets — navel, vulva, bum —
And the widening smile behind her embroidery.

She wears our babies like brooches on her abdomen.

Ivory & Water

If as a lonely bachelor who disapproves of women
You carve the perfect specimen out of snow-white ivory
And fall in love with your masterpiece and make love to her
(Or try to) stroking, fondling, whispering, kissing, nervous
In case you bruise ivory like flesh with prodding fingers,
And bring sea-shells, shiny pebbles, song-birds, colourful
    wild
Flowers, amber-beads, orchids, beach-balls as her presents,
And put real women's clothes, wedding rings, ear-rings, long
Necklaces, a brassière on the statue, then undress her
And lay her in your bed, her head on the feathery pillows
As if to sleep like a girlfriend, your dream may come true
And she warms and softens and you are kissing actual lips
And she blushes as she takes you in, the light of her eyes,
And her veins pulse under your thumb at the end of the
    dream
When she breaks out in a cold sweat that trickles into pools
And drips from her hair dissolving it and her fingers and
    toes,
Watering down her wrists, shoulders, rib-cage, breasts until
There is nothing left of her for anyone to hug or hold.

A Gift of Boxes

I

Rice grains between my chopsticks remind you of a flower.
I want to wash the hagi petals in my bowl, then balance
Before your lips an offering of crabs' brains on a shiso leaf
Which looks like a nettle from Ireland but does not sting.

II

We are completely out of proportion in the tea-house
Until we arrange around a single earthenware bowl
Ourselves, the one life, one meeting, a ribbon of water
And these makeshift ideograms of wet leaves, green tea.

III

You make a gift of boxes by putting boxes inside
Boxes, each one containing the Japanese air you breathe,
More and more of it in diminishing boxes, smallness
Condensing in the end to two boxes the size of tears.

IV

They have planted stones in the stone garden. If I sit still
The stones will take root in my imagination and grow.
You retire behind the fifteenth stone which I cannot see.
Whatever happens to a stone becomes its life, its flower.

Chenac

for Maurice Hayes

I

Today nothing happens in Chenac except for me
And you in the old bakery Maurice is rebuilding,
Rafters like branches, altar-wide hearth, cobwebby
Cubby-holes where yeast fizzed, bread cooled: our estate
Sweet blackberries and windfalls beside the marguerites;
Our guardians the spider out of the Book of Proverbs
That takes hold with her hands, and is in kings' palaces,
The centipede that shimmies where the cellar will be.

II

On twin pillars in St Martin's church bunches of grapes
And orioles repeat themselves and reach the starry sky
A child painted above the altar; until the bell
Recalls diminutive single sunflowers spouting here
And there, outcasts that escaped both sowing and harvest;
On the road to Épargnes where you can see our steeple
The buzzard with nowhere to perch but stubbly furrows
Flapping to his mate, a tangle of straw in his talons.

III

Accompanying us indoors before a rain-storm the lizard
Zig-zags into his cranny, who is exceeding wise
And makes his house in the rocks and therefore in this
house.

The Dry Cleaners

Poem Beginning with a Line of Raymond Carver

That time I tagged along with my dad to the dry cleaners
We bumped into Eurycleia whose afternoon-off it was
And bought her tea and watched her smooth the table-
Cloth and make her plate and doily concentric circles, then
Pick up cake-crumbs with a moistened finger, since to us
There was more to her than jugs and basins, hot water
And cold, bed-linen she tested against her cheek after
The rainy trek from clothes-line to airing cupboard. Once
She carried a lamp across the yard in front of me
And saw me to my bedroom and folded my clothes and
Smoothed them and hung them on a peg by my wooden bed
And pulled the door to by its silver handle and drew
Home the bolt with the leather strap and left me alone
Worried but cosy through the night under woolly blankets.
Eurycleia the daughter of Ops the son of Peisoner
Took care of me and haunts our wardrobe as the plastic bags
My clothes come back from the dry cleaners shrouded in.

The Fishing Party

Because he loves off-duty policemen and their murderers
Christ is still seen walking on the water of Lough Neagh,
Whose fingers created bluebottles, meadow-browns, red
Admirals, painted ladies, fire-flies, and are tying now
Woodcock hackles around the hooks, lamb's wool, badger
    fur

Until about his head swarm artificial flies and their names,
Dark Mackerel, Gravel Bed, Greenwell's Glory, Soldier
Palmer, Coachman, Water Cricket, Orange Grouse, Barm,
Without snagging in his hair or ceasing to circle above
Policemen turned by gunmen into fishermen for ever.

Ceasefire

I

Put in mind of his own father and moved to tears
Achilles took him by the hand and pushed the old king
Gently away, but Priam curled up at his feet and
Wept with him until their sadness filled the building.

II

Taking Hector's corpse into his own hands Achilles
Made sure it was washed and, for the old king's sake,
Laid out in uniform, ready for Priam to carry
Wrapped like a present home to Troy at daybreak.

III

When they had eaten together, it pleased them both
To stare at each other's beauty as lovers might,
Achilles built like a god, Priam good-looking still
And full of conversation, who earlier had sighed:

IV

'I get down on my knees and do what must be done
And kiss Achilles' hand, the killer of my son.'

The Scales

Thick as the snowflakes on a wintry day when God
Comes down as snow and shows mankind his arsenal,
Putting the winds to sleep, blanketing in snowdrifts
Hill-tops, rocky promontories, pasture, turning
Jetties and beaches white, melting for breakers only –
So flew the stones, a snowstorm of stones, and then
A thunderstorm, shields crunching against shields,
Spears splintering, death-rattles, battle cries, dead-
Lock all morning, until God the Father at noon
Adjusted his golden scales, and in them weighed
Death sentences, holding the beam up by the middle
To see whose destiny would wobble heavenwards,
Whose come to rest on life-supporting earth, and whose
Faces, when God thundered, would go white as snow.

The Mad Poet

When someone's afflicted with the itchy nirls
Or jaundice or religious fundamentalism,
You don't play tig with him: ditto the mad poet,
Head in the air, burping pomes, dootering about:

And if, like a wildfowler gawking at blackbirds,
He cope-carlies into a waterhole or heugh
And gulders 'Hi! dear readers! Help!' – do not
Swing him a life-line: sling him a deafie instead.

How do you know he isn't cowping accident-
ally on purpose (and *likes* it down there) just as
That head-the-ball Empedocles a header took
– In hot pursuit of immortality – into Etna?

It's still not clear what hurts him into verse, whether
He pissed on his father's ashes (in the urn) or
Thrappled his muse: at all events he is horn-daft
Like a bear bending the bars of his limitations.

His mad-dog shite has everyone – the poetry-buffs
And the iggerant – shit-scared: he grabbles you, then
He reads you to death, a leech cleeking your skin
Who won't drop off until he is boke-full of blood.

After Horace

We postmodernists can live with that human head
Stuck on a horse's neck, or the plastering of multi-
Coloured feathers over the limbs of assorted animals
(So that what began on top as a gorgeous woman
Tapers off cleverly into the tail of a black fish).

Since our fertile imaginations cannot make head
Or tail of anything, wild things interbreed with tame,
Snakes with birds, lambs with tigers. If a retired sailor
Commissions a picture of the shipwreck he survived,
We give him a cypress-tree because we can draw that.

To relieve the boredom we introduce to the woods
A dolphin, a wild boar to the waves. Ultimate post-
Modernists even in the ceramics department we
May have a vase in mind when we start, or a wine-jug,
But, look, as the wheel goes round, it ends up as a po.

Acknowledgements

The poems in this selection are taken from the following books, to whose publishers acknowledgement is made: *A Painted Field* (Picador, 1997) for Robin Robertson; *Nights in the Iron Hotel* (Faber and Faber, 1983), *Acrimony* (Faber and Faber, 1986), *Corona, Corona* (Faber and Faber, 1993) for Michael Hofmann; *Poems 1963–1983* (Salamander Press, 1985, Secker & Warburg, 1991), *Gorse Fires* (Secker & Warburg, 1991), *The Ghost Orchid* (Jonathan Cape, 1995) for Michael Longley.

Visit Penguin on the Internet
and browse at your leisure

- preview sample extracts of our forthcoming books
- read about your favourite authors
- investigate over 10,000 titles
- enter one of our literary quizzes
- win some fantastic prizes in our competitions
- e-mail us with your comments and book reviews
- instantly order any Penguin book

and masses more!

'To be recommended without reservation ... a rich and rewarding on-line experience' – Internet Magazine

www.penguin.co.uk

READ MORE IN PENGUIN

In every corner of the world, on every subject under the sun, Penguin represents quality and variety – the very best in publishing today.

For complete information about books available from Penguin – including Puffins, Penguin Classics and Arkana – and how to order them, write to us at the appropriate address below. Please note that for copyright reasons the selection of books varies from country to country.

In the United Kingdom: Please write to *Dept. EP, Penguin Books Ltd, Bath Road, Harmondsworth, West Drayton, Middlesex UB7 0DA*

In the United States: Please write to *Consumer Sales, Penguin USA, P.O. Box 999, Dept. 17109, Bergenfield, New Jersey 07621-0120*. VISA and MasterCard holders call 1-800-253-6476 to order Penguin titles

In Canada: Please write to *Penguin Books Canada Ltd, 10 Alcorn Avenue, Suite 300, Toronto, Ontario M4V 3B2*

In Australia: Please write to *Penguin Books Australia Ltd, P.O. Box 257, Ringwood, Victoria 3134*

In New Zealand: Please write to *Penguin Books (NZ) Ltd, Private Bag 102902, North Shore Mail Centre, Auckland 10*

In India: Please write to *Penguin Books India Pvt Ltd, 706 Eros Apartments, 56 Nehru Place, New Delhi 110 019*

In the Netherlands: Please write to *Penguin Books Netherlands bv, Postbus 3507, NL-1001 AH Amsterdam*

In Germany: Please write to *Penguin Books Deutschland GmbH, Metzlerstrasse 26, 60594 Frankfurt am Main*

In Spain: Please write to *Penguin Books S. A., Bravo Murillo 19, 1° B, 28015 Madrid*

In Italy: Please write to *Penguin Italia s.r.l., Via Felice Casati 20, I–20124 Milano*

In France: Please write to *Penguin France S. A., 17 rue Lejeune, F–31000 Toulouse*

In Japan: Please write to *Penguin Books Japan, Ishikiribashi Building, 2–5–4, Suido, Bunkyo-ku, Tokyo 112*

In South Africa: Please write to *Longman Penguin Southern Africa (Pty) Ltd, Private Bag X08, Bertsham 2013*

READ MORE IN PENGUIN

A SELECTION OF POETRY

American Verse
British Poetry since 1945
Caribbean Verse in English
Chinese Love Poetry
A Choice of Comic and Curious Verse
Contemporary American Poetry
Contemporary British Poetry
Contemporary Irish Poetry
English Poetry 1918–60
English Romantic Verse
English Verse
First World War Poetry
German Verse
Greek Verse
Homosexual Verse
Imagist Poetry
Irish Verse
Japanese Verse
The Metaphysical Poets
Modern African Poetry
New Poetry
Poetry of the Thirties
Scottish Verse
Surrealist Poetry in English
Spanish Verse
Victorian Verse
Women Poets
Zen Poetry

READ MORE IN PENGUIN

POETRY LIBRARY

Blake	Selected by W. H. Stevenson
Browning	Selected by Daniel Karlin
Burns	Selected by Angus Calder and William Donnelly
Byron	Selected by A. S. B. Glover
Clare	Selected by Geoffrey Summerfield
Coleridge	Selected by Richard Holmes
Donne	Selected by John Hayward
Dryden	Selected by Douglas Grant
Hardy	Selected by David Wright
Housman	Introduced by John Sparrow
Keats	Selected by John Barnard
Kipling	Selected by Craig Raine
Lawrence	Selected by Keith Sagar
Milton	Selected by Laurence D. Lerner
Pope	Selected by Douglas Grant
Rubáiyát of Omar Khayyám	Translated by Edward FitzGerald
Shelley	Selected by Isabel Quigly
Tennyson	Selected by W. E. Williams
Wordsworth	Selected by Nicholas Roe
Yeats	Selected by Timothy Webb

READ MORE IN PENGUIN

A SELECTION OF POETRY

James Fenton Out of Danger

A collection wonderfully open to experience – of foreign places, differences, feelings and languages.

U. A. Fanthorpe Selected Poems

'She is an erudite poet, rich in experience and haunted by the classical past ... fully at home in the world of the turbulent NHS, the decaying academies, and all the draughty corners of the abandoned Welfare State' – *Observer*

Craig Raine Clay. Whereabouts Unknown

'I cannot think of anyone else writing today whose every line is so unfailingly exciting' – *Sunday Times*

Marge Piercy Eight Chambers of the Heart

Marge Piercy's poetry is written to be read and spoken aloud, to move, provoke and entertain, on every subject under the sun from ecology to cats and cookery, to political, sexual and family relationships.

Joseph Brodsky To Urania
Winner of the 1987 Nobel Prize for Literature

Exiled from the Soviet Union in 1972, Joseph Brodsky has been universally acclaimed as the most talented Russian poet of his generation.

Paul Celan Selected Poems
Winner of the first European Translation Prize, 1990

'The English reader can now enter the hermetic universe of a German–Jewish poet who made out of the anguish of his people, things of terror and beauty' – *The Times Literary Supplement*

Geoffrey Hill Canaan

'Among our finest poets, Geoffrey Hill is at present the most European – in his Latinity, in his dramatization of the Christian condition, in his political intensity' – *Sunday Times*